THE CATECHETICAL EXPERIENCE

THE CATECHETICAL EXPERIENCE

JOHN F. MURPHY

HERDER AND HERDER

1968
HERDER AND HERDER NEW YORK
232 Madison Avenue, New York 10016

Nihil obstat: Brendan W. Lawlor, Censor Librorum
Imprimatur: ✝ Robert F. Joyce, Bishop of Burlington
December 28, 1967

Grateful acknowledgement is hereby made to The Newman
Press for permission to reprint a selection from *The Worship
of the Church,* by William O'Shea (Westminster, 1957).

Library of Congress Catalog Card Number: 68–19479
© 1968 by Herder and Herder, Inc.
Manufactured in the United States

CONTENTS

INTRODUCTION

In the fall of 1965, I began a journey with a new senior high school religion class, one that has affected me greatly. During that year I kept a journal of the class day by day which enabled me to trace my own thinking and that of the students as we moved along together. That journal provides the basis for this volume.

Two elements that year changed my approach to catechetics: the first was my willingness to explore and examine my own approaches and motives; the second was my willingness to be more open than before to the voices of my students.

In the planning stages for that year's work, the suggestion by Father Ronald Richardson, the other senior religion teacher, that we plan and work through a theme for the year, that we examine our approaches and goals, caught me up short somewhat. Frankly, my fairly successful attempts at teaching for the previous years had made me somewhat complacent and I had not realized what might be lacking.

The results of the planning session will show up in the journal itself. Equally important was a beginning from a teacher-centered and directed class to a student-centered approach, an approach that demanded a new look at the students themselves, the material used, and my role.

This transition from teacher-centered to student-centered opened a dimension whose full effects are still being felt in me. When a human being meets with another on the question of truth, there can develop a tension, a re-evaluation, a common search which unsettles, and yet gives life. It is the ever recurring idea of meeting Christ and being opened to a dimension outside of oneself occurring when we are forced to see beyond our own world and to go out to another's.

It is one thing to see another's world; it is another to accept it and become one with it. This is not new in teaching, yet it is always a revelation. In the teaching of religion we occasionally enter into the students' world, but too frequently we enter with our defenses up and our arguments ready. This year I entered and discovered anew the world of faith.

In discovering the world of faith, I did not find what I had expected and seen before—miniature Christians awaiting only the development of time. Rather I found young men who were continually discovering themselves and Christ, at an uneven pattern of growth. In truth they had had, in some cases, eleven years of previous religion instruction; but, in being true to themselves, they were searching out all their values in preparation for manhood.

I discovered that faith is more of a growth than I had believed; and I was concerned and, at times, frightened. Yet, fortunately, my fear did not reveal itself to the students who continued to ask and to challenge. Only slowly did I realize more and more the meaning of faith.

In the same process, I began to discover the role of the teacher, or perhaps better, his difficulties. My own concern and fears may have hindered my own work; yet the honesty and candor of the students made me realize the need for a risk, the risk of letting them open so that we could explore together the needs of the faith today.

What may cause some small surprise to some readers is the fact that these students, although not all, were continuing on to the college department of our seminary as hopeful students for the priesthood. I did not differentiate in the notes between those who elected to stay and those who chose to leave. My basic interest was in all these young men as Christians. Is a young man of seventeen or eighteen preparing for the priesthood immune from questions or challenges? I would hope not, considering the apostolic tradition which continues in conciliar debates. Peter and Paul searched and questioned. Grace builds as man grows. And the man is not a result of certitude, but of searching; and the meeting of man with Christ proceeds unevenly as the man learns to know himself, to achieve his own consciousness, his own identity.

This journal was not written for publication. The basic idea for it grew out of the idea of self-evaluation needed in a discussion approach with students. The value was in the fairly honest approach used. To read from class to class and month to month about one's own failings and difficulties and successes is to be made more and more aware of the difficulty of teaching and of the need for reflection.[1]

1. Cf. John F. Murphy, "A Catechetical Diary: Its Value and Development," in *The Living Light,* vol. 4, no. 3, pp. 83–87.

This was not a unique catechetical experience; it could be considered very commonplace. Yet it may have elements that can be seen by others which offer insights for them. We too frequently teach in a vacuum of our own experience. Occasionally we share one or two classes with another, yet we do not have enough knowledge of the actual day-to-day existence in the classroom. We tend to idealize our experiences, highlighting some days over others. Perhaps we are unaware of other teachers' difficulties in not having a complete lesson, in being interrupted, in not really covering the material, in having students not understand.

In catechetics today we should share with one another in our difficulties and our common drawbacks. From one experience such as this, perhaps others will be helped to go much further.

The notes reveal one class's approach to the world around them and my efforts with them to direct their thinking. I did not think everything was successful and my own reflections after another year and a half of teaching here would confirm this. Yet the experience happened and it cannot be erased. In much of our catechetical writing we talk of what should and could be done. *This is what was done.* Truth is not discovered in a vacuum. I discovered much about myself and my students, and I am thankful to them for all they contributed in being themselves. I apologize for my own failings.

The notes reveal one class's approach to the world around them and my efforts with them to direct their thinking. I did not think everything was successful and my own reflections after another year and a half of teaching here would confirm this. What I wanted to do and what I did were not the same. This

10

was a beginning for me and it has not ended. I realize that in offering these notes that there is the danger that some will feel they are being offered as a guide or model. That would be unfair and untrue to the reader, to the students I taught, and to myself. I am willing to share my experiences, to be open about my own techniques and problems and approaches, and to learn from others.

The movement in catechetics today to a student-centered approach, to helping students to see their own experiences as "revelatory," does not come easily nor is there any sure path. I realized that when I was teaching and I had difficulty in overcoming my own background. Perhaps it is in seeing what has been done, as with this class, that we can see where we should be going and how we will do it. I am still feeling the tension between what I want to do and what I am doing. The place for me to start is where I have been, and perhaps others will find they have been there with me.

St. Pius X Preparatory School
Uniondale, New York

NOTE

THE notes from this journal are given as written during that year with all the pressures of daily or weekly note-taking. As a result they are not a polished and finished account of a carefully analyzed situation.

In preparing the notes for publication, I decided against a re-writing of the actual notes. Also I have not included a detailed analysis of the classes day by day. That would involve a onesided view, my own. I felt that each reader should see the notes as they were written, and each reader could bring his own experiences and insights as a guide to understanding this particular experience. Some lapse in continuity may be evident in this approach, but perhaps even this discontinuity should be shared.

The notes do not reflect the humor and human element that were present in the class, yet the class could not have existed without them. They were present because the students were present to one another and to me.

Where necessary, I have included some explanatory notes or some brief comment to place some of the situations and comments in context.

THE CATECHETICAL EXPERIENCE

OUTLINE OF THE COURSE

RELIGION IV.[1]

SECTION 4A

TEXTS:

Constitution on the Liturgy, *Pacem in Terris,* Gospel of John.

BASIC THEME:

Community of man and God.

AIMS:

To develop in the students an understanding of the meaning of community, first natural and then Christian; to see its necessity; to help them develop the means of establishing community and to help them understand the means for community given by God and man.

GENERAL INTRODUCTION FOR STUDENTS:

A. Nature of man taken from literature they have read (with special relation to man's need for community).

1. This outline is a summary of the discussions I had with Father Ronald Richardson, who taught the other section of the senior year. It was written after we had talked on several occasions. I felt I needed some reminder of what we had said in order to keep my goals in mind.

The Pearl, Silas Marner, The Witness, A Separate Peace, The Lord of the Flies, King Lear, Our Town, etc.

B. In the Constitution on the Liturgy, have students discover references to community. Are they real? Why not?

C. Develop ideas from students on how community becomes meaningful and effective.

D. What are the aids in liturgy to making community? What is the responsibility of the individual to community formation?

E. Does community differ according to circumstances? Are different techniques and adaptations needed for community on different levels of culture, age?

F. It is hoped that students will develop ideas of some action in expressing community here first and possibly outside the area of St. Pius Preparatory School.

G. After some study of community as expressed in liturgy, students should begin to see relation of the community of the people of God to the world around them. This could lead to *Pacem in Terris.*

AIDS AND DEVICES:

A. Films, contemporary secular films which point up man's need for community, e.g. "On the Waterfront," Grail film on social justice (must call about that).

B. Elizabeth Reid of the Grail, connected with the U.N., may be able to cooperate in terms of a visit to the U.N. or a talk here.

C. Check on resource people who can visit here.

D. Explore possibility of visits to certain areas of community interest in the county.

FIRST SEMESTER

Report on Class Discussion and Reaction
as of This Date (*October 10*)

THE class has met ten times.[1] That, however, included the opening day of school and that first period was only twenty minutes. Also, on September 26 we discussed the forthcoming visit of the Pope and on October 6 we discussed the actual trip. In terms of the topic of community, we have had seven classes.

The following is an attempt to trace the growth or development of the topic in the last seven sessions on community.[2]

1. Religion class meets three times a week. The days for this class were Monday, Wednesday, and Thursday. In the 4B section there were 34 students, arranged in six rows facing the teacher's desk. Each period is approximately 40 minutes.

This following year I have tried a new arrangement with a third-year class. I have broken up the class into two groups, evenly divided in terms of leadership and participation. On one day I take one group; the second group the next day; on the third day I take the whole class. The seating for the small groups is more informal and the level of participation has improved considerably. The students not involved on the first or second day work in the library.

2. In the journal I rarely mentioned students by name, probably because I knew them well and did not need the reminder. In this printing I have removed the few names that were in the notes. If this were a novel or personal history, names would be essential. I felt, however, that inclusion of a few names would not be helpful to the reader. Also the individual student has a right to speak freely without being reported by name to the general public.

Monday, September 13 and *Thursday, September 16.* Wednesday's class did not meet because of the visit of the bishop to the school.[1]

In the opening classes, for which I did not take notes, the class discussed the idea of man as taught or seen in *The Lord of the Flies, Silas Marner, The Pearl,* and from a statement on his own life by Albert Schweitzer. The ideas coming from the students were that man was evil, that he needed other men, that man's nature involved being with others, that man was happiest when he went outside of himself. (One student pointed out that the Birdman of Alcatraz needed his pets in order to get outside of himself when in solitary confinement. Another student pointed out that the inventor of the carbine did the design when in solitary confinement, and that going outside himself in creative work helped him survive the punishment of being completely alone.)

From this we proceeded to go into the nature of community. The students indicated that a community was a group of people with a common goal, united in some fashion. It was not necessarily a town or a neighborhood, although the word *community* is used there. When asked for examples of community that they had experienced, they mentioned basketball games here at the school, Holy Week services here, the concelebrated Mass. When asked to mention groups that seem to have the experience or sign of community, they mentioned the Ku Klux Klan, the John Birch Society, the Muslims.

1. Traditionally, the ordinary of the diocese has come to open the school year.

Monday, September 20. On this day we reviewed the elements of community and asked what the communities they have mentioned provided for the member of the community and what the individual member had to give. They pointed out from the basketball games they attended that they received

security by being a member of the group

support for their own feelings

accomplishment when the group succeeded.

This they felt was true at the times of basketball games and school elections. They felt, in turn, that the individual had to share with others in community in order to receive the benefits. Also, it had to be pointed out that the members of a "good" community had to respect the rights of each, i.e., the personal rights, e.g., *The Lord of the Flies.* The students then proceeded, after I had summarized some of their previous thinking, to indicate that the Christian community was generally not effective now, at least not as effective as the KKK, John Birch, Muslims.

Wednesday, September 22. My notes for the Wednesday class read as follows:

Communities – KKK, John Birch, Muslims

/

Goal – Drive

/

Christian community generally not effective

The proposed questions for Wednesday were as follows:

What are the elements mitigating Christian community?

What are the elements which would really, if possible, form a community?

(I had intended to have the students lead to a point where I could introduce the idea of God intervening in human society, its effect, the use of liturgy as a sign and force of community, and the resulting action from it.[1])

On this day I went from my proposed questions to a new one.[2] The previous Monday evening I visited St. Agnes parish in downtown Brooklyn which has a large Puerto Rican and Negro population now in addition to the older, more established Italian-Irish group. One of our joint plans here is to have the boys visit the parish in order to gain some idea of urban problems of community and the relation of the Christian to these problems.

At the beginning of this class I asked the students how many of them would be really interested in helping to form a Christian community in a parish that included Puerto Ricans and Negroes. In terms of their honest answers, most had no positive reaction. It had no appeal to them generally.[3] The idea was that they did

1. I saw later that I wanted to make too great a leap in my plans by leading the students too quickly to an "answer." In seeing the relationships myself, I was forgetting how students think; also I did not consider the difference between my own knowledge and background, and their development at this point. My concern should have been to develop and explore, rather than to solve by my answers. The "right" answer is important; what is also important is that the students, if possible, help make the path to it with the teacher's help. It is a fine line to walk. Fortunately, in this situation, another development occurred.

2. In actuality, lesson plans should be followed. On-the-spot developments, however, should not be ignored. Frequently, the best made plans will be altered because of special situations or because a new idea has come since the plans were made.

3. These students live in a white, suburban, generally middle-class diocese. Their contacts with urban slums were almost completely negli-

not care. I asked what would be the reactions of Jehovah Witnesses in the same situation. One student answered that they would be eager. When questioned why, he answered that the JW took the Gospel literally. I asked him if we did. He said, rather spontaneously, no. I mentioned the text "Teach all nations." The student indicated that we might not go to all people, even if the JW's did. One student, at the end of the period, said there was a lack of Christianity in Catholicism.[2]

Thursday, September 23. On this day we reviewed quickly the points of the previous class. My questions for the day were:

1. Why don't we have a Christian community when the JW's do?
2. Why aren't we concerned about our neighbor really?
3. What are the elements of the Christian life that would reform us and make us a Christian community?
4. Do we have an obligation to form a community?

The answers to these questions were something as follows: The JW's love more; we were told not to involve ourselves directly with others; we did not have the idea of the priesthood

---

gible, as I discovered later. My reaction of surprise was markedly changed after they had visited the slums, had been opened to a new world, and had positively reacted to the apostolate being done there. Their reaction was not one of limited Christianity as much as limited vision.

2. The awareness of the deficiences of Catholicism is not surprising at this age, when questions about all values are raised. The willingness to look more objectively at the Church in pilgrimage with its failings is probably one of the requisites of growth. The acceptance of reality, even if it seems onesided at first, is a major step which can be balanced by other factors.

of the laity; we are baptized but not committed; I have no reason to worry about others, why should I be bothered?; buck-passing.

What really works? Suggested answers (without enthusiasm) were the Eucharist, confession, sacred scripture.

One student felt that in order to change we need a direct contact with Christ, a personal relationship with Christ; we need a relation with God if we are to have a relation with one another.

Another student felt that the average Christian was like the average guy.

The final point, from one student, was rather pessimistic. Perhaps Catholicism isn't any good.

On that note I prepared for the next class. After discussion with Fr. Richardson I decided to try to lead the class into revelation (not as a *deus ex machina*, but as a fact).

Monday, September 25. Devoted to the forthcoming trip of Pope Paul VI.

Wednesday, September 27. My notes read as follows:

I. Class review. Present state of Christians; some type of indifference; we don't care; we, as Christians, are not very different from other people; we avoid responsibility; we pass the buck; we are baptized, but we are not committed; we lack concept of priesthood of laity.

In order to change we need a personal relationship to Christ, a direct contact with God.

II. Questions and general direction:

The other day I asked what elements in the Christian life would help form community. How did God intend to help man form a community? Why does man have difficulty in establishing a community? Does man have to form a community?

God intervenes in man's world. What do we need? Return to the source. God!! OT People of God. How did they react? What did God provide? a form of unity: a meal. Is there any group from whom we can learn who experienced the truth and did not use it. Also what would be the reason for having a Christian community (trying to get them to see the work of the apostolate in influencing the world, e.g., *Pacem in Terris*).

What does the Christian have in common with the Jew?

Review elements of community?

What is the function of the Christian community?

Why and how a personal contact with Christ in the community?

What is really effective in forming a Christian?

Where does one begin to effect Christian changes in the community?

What can we as a group of Christians do to express our sense of community here? (at school) this mark period?

What does the liturgical revival have to do with community? Is it effective? Why? Why not?[1]

In the actual class we had on Wednesday we started off with what man has to do in order to be involved in community. He has to forget himself. The students said that man does not go outside of himself and his own particular, narrow community because of fear of rejection, or responsibility, and because he feels secure with his own group. We arrived at this point by discussing new people in their neighborhoods, especially a boy their own

1. Outlines in a teacher's notebook can be overly ambitious, especially this day's notes. Perhaps, for myself, it is often a way to think myself out.

27

age who must strive to get into community rather than have the boys themselves go out to bring him in. (An interesting point of development here, which I did not see at the time, and did not develop would be the fact that a boy coming into a new community *seeks* to become one with others.)

In order to form a community, one student said, you need a leader, and this would be true of the Christian community also, e.g., Pope John XXIII.

The common goal of the Christian community would be cooperation and charity. Interestingly enough, the idea of cooperation was directed primarily to the Christian community alone. No mention was made of the Christian community going out to non-Christians, until it was pointed out that this concept was not included in their ideas.

At this point I interrupted or changed the direction to discuss the people of God in the OT (this class has not had a strong OT background). I brought in the idea of a community having law, goal, leader, and this was applied to the Jewish community before and after the exodus. The parallel to the NT community was indicated.

Towards the end of the class one student said the present-day parish community in suburban Long Island was too large. The novelty of Christianity had worn off.

Thursday, September 30. We reviewed yesterday's class. My point was to direct the class to Christ as leader and former of a Christian and the Christian community. It was much more directed by me than earlier classes.

I began with the problem of the large parishes and the difficulty of establishing community under those circumstances. I asked them how long it would take to form a community. One answer was about two or three years for the average parish on Long Island. How would they go about it? One suggested the homilies of the priests. Another hit upon the idea of something like the Legion of Mary: this evolved into also the idea of a nucleus of perhaps twenty to twenty-five committed men. When I asked the students how these men would become committed Christians, they seemed somewhat perplexed. I finally gave them a simple answer—Christ. This caught them off guard and I could tell by their reaction that they had not thought of that (oddly enough, it was suggested by a student who had earlier said that a strong personal relation to Christ was necessary—cf. September 23).

After that sank in, I put a diagram on the board,

God
/ | \
man – man – man

indicating that man has a relationship to God and then to others. Man's nature is that he needs social relations. Yet he needs God in order to react fully and openly to other men. God reacts to man and enables man to react to other men. (During this time we have read a short passage each class from John's first epistle and now we have just started John's gospel.) One student pointed out that some men have loved man without a structured relationship (my terminology) to God. I pointed out that often

29

they are men of extremely exceptional personalities. The average man would need God's help and also God works through all men, even if not formally as we know it.

This led to a question of the liturgy and of the Mass, in particular. Without leading the obvious point, I asked one student why he went to Mass and what it was for. He said Mass was to get to heaven and that was all. It held little interest for the student and he could have done without it. A surprising number of students also admitted that the Mass meant not much more to them. One or two qualified their statements by saying the present structure of the Mass.[1]

(I have just remembered one class where a student said a Christian community would have to be involved in civil rights, etc. Another student said hold it. That was too much for him.)

Monday, October 4. Visit of Pope Paul VI to U.N. No school.

Wednesday, October 6. Discussion of Pope Paul's visit and speech at the U.N. Surprisingly to me, some of the boys, who were free at the time, did not watch the Pope at the U.N. I did comment unfavorably at that, perhaps too critically. For my part I felt a disappointment that they did not share my enthusiasm.

1. Although we had full participation in the Mass according to the rules at that time, the structure of the liturgy still left much to be desired in terms of the adolescents' reactions. While objectively they knew and understood a great deal about worship, subjectively for some it was a difficult time. It raises the whole question of habit and personal response on the adolescent level, an area still being explored.

This applies to only part of the class; I also feel I should not have been as strong in my disapproval.

Thursday, October 7. New York State Scholarship Exam; no class for seniors.

Monday, October 11. In my preparation notes for this class I indicated the following: Review the role of Christ in forming men. Christ forms men through what instrument? How did he form the early Christians? How would you go about forming Christian men to form a Christian community? Cf. people in the desert, in the promised land? (I was looking for a passover reference.) Did it work? They knew him in the breaking of bread. What did Christ do? Meal! Why? Is it real? What other source do we have? Other Christians. Sacred scripture.[1]

While I was discussing this class with Fr. Arthur Anderson (a member of the religion department), he suggested that I stress the formation of the Jews in the desert as a community with the following points: common need, adversity, heritage with a rallying point in their leader Moses. The passover was to keep alive their deliverance.

In the class I discovered my own questions would not provoke too much discussion. Perhaps it was because we had discussed much of it earlier. I proceeded to the question of the Jews in the OT. Again it was evident that the lack of OT background

1. In retrospect, I could see that my questions were too inclusive and wide. Also I realized how much more I needed to know about the background of my students before heading into certain areas.

was something of a hindrance. From their somewhat limited knowledge of the exodus, they were able to arrive at the idea of a common heritage, adversity, goal, leader, food. They understood the idea of the promised land vaguely, were more clear on Moses, the manna. When I asked them to apply all this to the present Christian community, they remarked that we today do not have much adversity and this causes a problem in forming a common bond among Christians in this area. In terms of the early Christians they felt that the early Christians knew Christ more directly and hence had a closer bond (in terms of "Christ in the sacraments"—this is interesting).

When I asked why did Christ have to establish a community, they answered that it was too hard for the early Christian to do it alone and also to save us from what had kept us apart in the first place (this indicates to me that I have much work to do on the idea people of God—the view that we are one by God's plan. The last answer in my notes was that we need a community to gain happiness, although this isn't explained).

In the discussion I tried to have them see the difficulties Christ experienced in forming a community. The comment that evolved from one student was that Christ didn't have a ball.

Wednesday, October 13. We reviewed the previous class. I pointed out that Christ established a community because it was too hard for people to do it alone, his people needed a leader, needed something in common, needed a way of coming together to remember what had been done, what was their heritage. I asked them what the Jews did and still do to help keep alive their spirit. I was hoping to lead them to the passover.

It was with great difficulty that we arrived anywhere near the passover. I brought out the idea of the passover and asked what was the reason for the Jews celebrating the passover each year. This evoked the responses that it reminded them of what God had done, it made them happy, it helped them renew themselves. Yet underneath there was not much response to the idea that it was really a significant experience for the Jewish community. When I mentioned that it was a way of reminding the Jews that God loved them, the response was to ask what was so special about the Jews. I also got the answer that the "Jews have this stuff in the Bible." What was so special about that?[1]

It was at this point that I decided I had better go into some OT background with this class. Also I began a discussion on the question of the Jews as the chosen people, and on the Bible as the record of salvation history.

Thursday, October 14. This class took up a discussion of two items.[2]

1. The forcefulness of this answer in terms of its bluntness struck home. Teaching the Bible or working with salvation history is a major problem in catechetics today. This student's observation did not reflect every student's approach, but it did make a point on the effectiveness of the revival of Bible and liturgy on some of our students.

2. One of the perennial problems of teaching is the interruption of a topic because of announcements that are important but take the class away from the regular material. The problem of continuity is further complicated, e.g., in discussions that are going very strongly and are stopped by the bell. If the class does not meet for two or three days, it is

1. On Thursday, October 28, Sr. Thomas Marie, a Trinitarian sister from a Negro and Puerto Rican parish in Brooklyn, would speak to them about the work of the Christian community in the area she was working in.
2. For this mark period they were to write an essay on
   a. the significance of Pope Paul's visit to the UN, or
   b. their ideas for forming a Christian community, or
   c. how the Jews were formed into a community as found in the Book of Exodus.

That would be handed in October 21, Thursday, the day before the close of the mark period. I assigned no length but left that to their discretion.

I then began a discussion of the Bible including literary forms in the Bible. At the end of the period I could see the need for some notes for them to work with.

Monday, October 18. I handed out notes on salvation history in the OT (see below). On this day I discussed creation and Adam. It is interesting to note that some of the students were surprised at the gratuitous nature of creation. In discussion on the sin of Adam and Eve I pointed out how man was not satisfied with his own humanity, but wished to be something other than man, or rather more than man, and that his perhaps was the meaning of the first sin.[1] I included some questions on the literary form in the first twelve chapters of Genesis. The class was generally very

---

sometimes frustrating to realize that you cannot regain the enthusiasm of that discussion in the next class.

1. I realize now how much more has been written on original sin.

absorbed in this class, although it included much lecture. (An interesting sidelight was that one student fell sound asleep right in front of me, in spite of the fact that some students said it was an excellent class.)

SALVATION HISTORY — THE OLD TESTAMENT
(God loves us and reveals himself to us)

1. Salvation History
    a. "narrative of the progressive saving encounters of God with man . . ." "the record that sees God revealing himself in the historical fact."
    b. preparatory (OT) and definitive encounters (NT)
2. Themes and events in God's preparation for Christ
    a. Creation and Adam
        i. gift of God to man (Genesis)
        ii. man's rejection (Genesis)
        iii. God's persistence (Genesis and entire Bible)
    b. Covenant
        i. original meaning for Bedouin tribes
        ii. God approaches man through Abraham (Genesis 17, 1–8)
        iii. God forms an agreement with his people through Moses (Exodus 24ff., Deuteronomy 5, 6ff.)
        iv. The signs of the covenant
        v. The covenant in practice (Joshua, Judges, Kings)
        vi. God speaks through his prophets and promises a new covenant (Jeremiah 31, 31–34)
    c. People of God
        i. God calls Abraham to be the Father of many nations (Genesis)
        ii. God forms his people on Mount Sinai into a nation (Exodus and Deuteronomy)
        iii. The kingdom on earth is formed (Kings)
        iv. The prophets give a vision of a new kingdom (Isaiah)

35

d. Exodus
  i. Abraham called from his land to a new place (Genesis)
  ii. Moses leads his people from Egypt to the promised land (Exodus)
  iii. The passover—the sign of the exodus

Wednesday, October 20. This period was spent on the idea of covenant as found on the mimeographed sheet. It was only partially successful since I either attempted too much or I didn't have all the material with me or adequately organized.

Thursday, October 21. On this day I summarized the question of covenant from Abraham to Christ, lecturing most of the time. It included discussion of the kingdom and the response of the Jewish people to the terms of the covenant and the prophet's admonitions. I applied this to the NT times, including a reference to our keeping of the new covenant.

On this day I collected the students' essays. Almost all were in on time. I asked the students to grade themselves. They were surprised, but did what I asked. In reading the papers I found them to be better than average. Some obviously put in a great deal of work. In general they are coming slowly to an abstract concept of community. Much of what they wrote shows not too much in the idea of their own personal involvement yet, although there are indications of it.

Monday, October 25. I talked about the papers that the students had written. I left all the papers in the desk so that students could read what the others had written if they wished. I have not checked up on this matter, although I know a number have read one student's paper which contained his ideas on the revision of the Mass (he's been writing it for two years and it certainly fit into the idea of community). On this day the school newspaper was being distributed. Several of the editors were in the class and they were excused. The class was somewhat broken apart by the comments on their papers and the distribution of the school paper towards the end of the period. I allowed the students to read the paper when it was delivered to the room.

Wednesday, October 27. Unfortunately, I don't recall this class. I know I mentioned that Sr. Thomas Marie, a Trinitarian sister from a Puerto Rican and Negro parish in downtown Brooklyn,[1] would be coming to speak to them the next day. I think that I also spoke on the question of the people of God in the OT.

Thursday, October 28. The two senior religion classes met together in the cafeteria. Sister Thomas Marie spoke to them for nearly twenty-five minutes about the Negro and Puerto Rican communities in Brooklyn, their needs and problems, the work of the Church, and so forth. At three o'clock, the end of the period, those students who wished to leave or had to, left. About forty out of the eighty remained, most of them for forty-five minutes, asking questions ranging from the relevance of the

1. These notes do not include all the outside planning and thinking that went on day by day. In our concern for contacts with other communities, we felt the need to bring in other people. Somewhere along the line we began to make arrangements that appear in the notes rather unexpectedly, e.g., Sr. Thomas Marie's appearance and the class Masses the following semester.

Church to this community, to drug addiction, school dropouts, community projects, war on poverty. The general reaction of the students was very enthusiastic.

Monday, November 1. Holy day and school holiday.

Wednesday, November 3. This period was spent discussing Sr. Thomas Marie's talk of the previous week. (It was unfortunate that we did not have a class sooner. The general reaction to the talk was good, but the ideas were not fresh in the minds of the students and they were groping for specific responses. When I noticed this, I turned the questioning in another direction.)

I asked the students why the Church was so involved in St. Ann's parish in Brooklyn. They answered that the people there show more need for the Church but have less actual reaction to the Church. What they sensed was that Sr. Thomas Marie knew that each person has his own value, that each person needs help. The work of the Church in that parish was to help each person there to know his own value. There was more of a sense of apostolate in that parish. I then asked them whether their parish shows any needs that would cause the parish to be apostolic. I then gave the answers (this now I see was a mistake since it could have been evoked from the students). They sensed that their own parishes had many more people going to church. I asked them if that necessarily meant that the parishioners were good Catholics. I then proceeded to point out some difficulties—numbers not going to the sacraments, CCD work in certain areas, generally status quo life.

38

Thursday, November 4. This class began with a few words to the students who were going to St. Ann's parish on Saturday, November 6, to participate in a teenage Mass.[1] All together, thirteen boys from both classes would go. The remainder of the class was devoted to my summation of the salvation history NT outline, completing all the lectures for a while in the class. Since I have not come to passover yet, I will use that as a point of departure for liturgy next week.

Saturday, November 6. The Mass was held in the basement of St. Ann's church. The folding chairs were set around three sides of the altar, the celebrant facing the community. On this occasion, representatives of the high-school Catholic Interracial Councils were present, along with many sisters, a few brothers, students from Cathedral College in Brooklyn (another preparatory seminary), and our students. In addition, there were teenagers from St. Ann's parish, although I could not myself tell who were the parishioners. Two Negro students acted as lector and music director. The music consisted of folk hymns. There was an offertory procession, homily. The general reaction of our students was that this was a real experience of community in liturgy. They were very moved. After the Mass they mixed with

1. Fr. Richardson and I had talked over the possibility of students visiting the inner city, e.g., downtown Brooklyn, in order to know another society and culture and to see community in a different setting. For our own students, slums are non-existent and they do not have the opportunity generally to visit them. The curates in St. Ann's parish in Brooklyn, Fathers Tom McCabe and Gerry Cannon, had agreed to help us. Our contact also with Sr. Thomas Marie made this parish a logical choice.

many of those present, but tended to stay mostly by themselves and with the Cathedral students. One of the curates mentioned that it might be possible next month to have a discussion after the Mass (then the sisters and the representatives of the interracial councils would not be present and the number would be less and our students would have to encounter the parishioners more directly).

Monday, November 8. My preparation notes for this class had the following: talk about assignment due next week. Questions: have students talk about experience in St. Ann's. What does it show you about liturgy and community? What are effects supposedly? What is liturgy attempting to do, with what techniques or persons? Read a section of the Constitution on the Liturgy.

In class I asked for a volunteer to talk about the experience. There was hesitation. I called on one student, well balanced, popular with all groups in the class, and a leader. He started off with the neighborhood as a slum. He found the church building better than expected. He noted the Negro commentator and music leader. The music, folk hymns, impressed him. He said he experienced a great sense of community. The Mass definitely impressed him. He enjoyed the hootenanny and expressed disappointment that he hadn't seen more of the neighborhood. He noted that perhaps we did not see the people as they really are since it was a social situation.

I then asked all the students who had been present at the Mass what caused the sense of community. The first answer was the surprise—"ourselves." Upon questioning, they said it was due to the spirit of the people present. The next answer was the location with the people gathered in a church basement close to the temporary altar. One student felt a great sense of meal. Another pointed out the role of the celebrant, his openness to the people, the way he said the greetings to the people. One felt the public inclusion of intentions at the commemoration of the living and the dead helped considerably. I continued the questioning regarding any other elements and the last one brought up by the students was the Eucharist. I pointed out to them that they brought this one up last. (I didn't go into the significance of this fact, but perhaps will later.) I then wanted them to see the role of the scriptures in forming community, so I proceeded to ask them for another element that helped community. I went back to the OT and the idea of Moses and his people. I asked them what else Moses did to bring the people together (hoping that they would see Moses' words. Perhaps if I had talked about Mount Sinai, they might have seen the connection with Moses telling the Law to the Jews). Finally, after they had suggested the offertory procession, the dialogue of priest and people, I mentioned scripture as the Liturgy of the Word. Several, who consider themselves budding liturgists, were taken aback that they had not thought of it. The bell concluded the period.

Wednesday, November 10. I reviewed rather quickly the previous class and then turned to the Constitution on the Liturgy. I had read it through again and selected key paragraphs to work with (those dealing with general principles). I had them read the second paragraph and give me the key ideas, which I then put on the blackboard. I insisted on answers from the text. Then

41

I went into what effect the Mass had at St. Ann's. One student said a commitment to each other. Then I asked what was the effect of daily Mass. Some had no idea. One said it occasionally made you conscious of others. Another said you meet Christ in Mass and after Mass, he is left in chapel. One said after four years of Mass, it was "too much."

Part of that class I asked what was the difference between a Peter, Paul, and Mary concert and a hootenanny Mass. I think that was when I got the answer about commitment in St. Ann's. I could sense towards the end of this class that some were finding difficulty bringing together paragraph 2[1] of the constitution with their own ideas and experiences of the Mass in general.

Monday, November 15. This class started with a review of what they had said last week. I asked them what the effect of the

1. "(2) For it is through the liturgy, especially the divine Eucharistic Sacrifice, that 'the work of our redemption is exercised.' The liturgy is thus the outstanding means by which the faithful can express in their lives, and manifest to others, the mystery of Christ and the real nature of the true Church. It is of the essence of the Church that she be both human and divine, visible and yet invisibly endowed, eager to act and yet devoted to contemplation, present in this world and yet not at home in it. She is all these things in such a way that in her the human is directed and subordinated to the divine, the visible likewise to the invisible, action to contemplation, and this present world to that city yet to come, which we seek (cf. Hebrews 13, 14). Day by day the liturgy builds up those within the Church into the Lord's holy temple, into a spiritual dwelling for God (cf. Ephesians 2, 21–22)—an enterprise which will continue until Christ's full stature is achieved (cf. Ephesians 4, 13). At the same time the liturgy marvelously fortifies the faithful in their capacity to preach Christ. To outsiders the liturgy thereby reveals the Church as a sign raised above the nations (cf. Isaiah 11, 12). Under this sign the scattered sons of God are being gathered into one (cf. John 11, 52) until there is one fold and one shepherd (cf. John 10, 16)."

Mass was. Then I asked what was the relationship between Mass and class, hoping to see some relationship between the bond of unity in the Eucharist and the interaction of people in school. We received many answers but few hit upon the idea of unity through the Eucharist expressed in everyday activities. One or two mentioned the idea of Mass as a sort of spiritual recharge, a feeling of contentment, and possibly some effect of persons outside of Mass. Some stressed again the idea of boredom of daily Mass. I sensed that perhaps I was not heading with the right questions, so I tried to get them to see the relationship of action and praying. One student did mention that we worship at Mass, and this was an interesting development in that it showed a God-directed action or involvement. I pointed out that the students were talking about what they got, not what they gave.

I asked what Fr. Gannon had said at St. Ann's about Mass and action, and one student pointed out that it was necessary to go forth, to respond in terms of what you had done.

(After class some students protested that I had been unfair, that it is impossible to have community as a result of Mass every day—it was too frequent. One student felt that community came before liturgy and that liturgy was not a prime factor in forming community. I realized how much would have to be rethought in order to have the students see the Eucharist not only as sign, but as sign effecting what it signifies. Some students seem more concerned about sign *only,* in contrast to the earlier training I had with its emphasis on effect only, rather than sign.[1])

1. The whole question of daily Mass on the high-school level has been somewhat difficult. At the time this class was given the students had class from 8:50 A.M. to 11:40 A.M. and then community Mass. Students'

Wednesday, November 17. My thoughts on this class came out after discussion with Fr. Richardson. We both felt there was a need for some introduction of dogma in terms of the Eucharist. My feeling was that the class should be helped in its understanding of the Mass by some rethinking and some introduction of material on the Eucharist. I prepared for the class by reading some material of Fr. Bernard Häring in his book *A Sacramental Spirituality,* just published. As I read through, I prepared the following notes for class: We have been exploring the relationship of community and Eucharist. The difficulty seems to lie in the idea of Eucharist. What is the relationship between liturgy and ethics? What is the idea of a sacrament? What about sign and effect? Texts from 1 Corinthians and John 6. The idea of covenant and response. What is the Eucharist from the constitution? What is liturgy? Idea of reverence.

In the class itself, I used some material from Fr. Häring's book. We discussed the meaning of the word *Eucharist* in terms of thanksgiving. I asked what thanksgiving implied, and by questioning arrived at the idea that a person who gives thanks tries also to live up to the person he is thanking—that there is a corollary between giving thanks for what someone has done and

---

lunch hour began then at 12:20 P.M. For many students, attention at Mass was affected by the unvarying time of Mass each day, following four class periods. At present, a new system has been introduced: three days a week the high-school students must attend either the community Mass at 11:40 A.M., or one scheduled at 8:00 A.M. If they attend the latter, they have a study period at 11:40. This change, plus the introduction of class Masses on occasion, has alleviated the problem of monotony of Mass the same period each day. On the other two days there is a concelebrated Mass which all students must attend.

44

continuing to be appreciative of that person by the way we treat that person. The idea of response came into play in terms of thanksgiving. The scripture texts helped the students see the idea of unity and of life. I did not go into the question of the presence of Christ or grace in too much detail. The class was rather occupied with the above.

Thursday, November 18. Seniors left for retreat at Gonzaga Retreat House, Monroe, New York.

Wednesday, November 24. (The seniors did not have religion class again until the Wednesday of Thanksgiving week.)

I asked the class for their general reaction to their retreat and then proceeded to the material for the day. I made some brief comment on the question of boredom in Eucharist and related it to the idea that perhaps we cannot always have excitement in liturgy. I did not open the class to discussion on frequency of Eucharist since it is not a point for discussion in view of the established custom here at this time.

I asked them to look at paragraph 47 of the Constitution on the Liturgy[1] to see how the council describes the Eucharist. I placed the key ideas on the board. Students pointed out that the

1. "(47) At the Last Supper, on the night when he was betrayed, our Saviour instituted the Eucharistic Sacrifice of his body and blood. He did this in order to perpetuate the sacrifice of the cross throughout the centuries until he should come again, and so to entrust to his beloved spouse, the Church, a memorial of his death and resurrection: a sacrament of love, a sign of unity, a bond of charity, a paschal banquet in which Christ is consumed, the mind is filled with grace, and a pledge of future glory is given to us."

Eucharist includes death and resurrection. Also that it is a memorial. After the ideas were on the board, I asked what was the difference between the passover celebration (one student had pointed out that it united the Jews, reminded them of obligation to God, and recalled an event that was) and the Eucharistic celebration. One student pointed out that the Eucharist is involved in something that in some way *is*. Also indicated Mass is sacrifice of the Church from *Unde et memores*. The class ended. In my notes for the day I indicated the future direction of the class—into the text of the Mass for an understanding of the Eucharistic celebration—then to a view of other sacraments, then the relation or effect of liturgy on community, to role of Church in society—ultimately to *Pacem in Terris*.

Monday, November 29. At this class I gave out the first page of the mimeographed notes (see extract below) on the meaning of the Mass taken from the book *The Worship of the Church,* by William O'Shea. After we had read through the page, I put on the board three points: (1) Do this in commemoration of me, (2) This is my body, this is my blood, (3) Offer *Unde et Memores*. I pointed out the relation between what Fr. O'Shea wrote and the three points. The class was attentive generally and responded to the ideas.

THE MEANING OF THE MASS

"Do this for a commemoration of me." That is what the Mass is first of all: a rite dedicated to commemorating and recalling Christ. It is essentially the Lord's own Supper, a Supper that is at the same time a Sacrifice. The Mass is not merely a subjective commemoration but an objective one, and it is not only a commemoration of Christ but of His whole redeeming work. "As often as you eat this bread and drink this chalice you proclaim the death of the Lord until he comes again" (1 Cor. 11, 26). A commemoration: we mean by that a sacred action which recalls, re-presents the work of salvation as it once took place in the past and brings it into the here and now. It is what we call a mystery. In that mystery Christ is present and operating. The work that He does is His redeeming passion, his transitus from this world to the Father, a transitus accomplished by His Passion, Death, Resurrection and Ascension. By His suffering and Death "He gave His life as a ransom for many," entered into conflict with the demon and vanquished him, and led a redeemed humanity through suffering and death to victory and glory. With His own blood He sealed the new and eternal Covenant and, passing into the Holy of Holies, obtained eternal redemption for us. (Cf. Heb. 9, 11.) He was the true Paschal Lamb whose blood delivered His people from Egypt, who died and lives again and who is the Bridegroom of the eternal wedding feast with the Spouse He has purchased for Himself. In this way He inaugurated the new creation.

On the night before He died, Christ left to His Church as His memorial the Supper that is a Sacrifice. By eating and drinking of this Sacrifice the Church is gathered together into one, eats and drinks of its own redemption, enters into the great redemptive mystery of the Passion, Death and Resurrection of her Lord. By this Memorial that is a Sacrifice, men of all times and all nations are able to take part in that great act of Christ which is His Paschal mystery.

But the Mass is not merely a Supper, nor merely the commemoration of a Sacrifice that has taken place in the past; it is itself a Sacrifice, the Sacrifice that Christ has left to His beloved Bride the Church. His Sacrifice is the Sacrifice of the Church; the Sacrifice of Christ to His heavenly Father is made through the hands of the priest. This much has always been clearly understood and believed, but that the Mass is at the same time the Sacrifice of the Church has been lost sight of to a great extent. Because it was necessary to defend

47

the Sacrifice itself against the reformers, and to emphasize that the Mass was a real Sacrifice, theologians concentrated on that aspect to the exclusion of its corollary: the Sacrifice of Christ is also the Sacrifice of the Church.

In more recent times, and largely as a result of the liturgical movement, attention is being given once again to that complete presentation of the doctrine of the Eucharist which sees the Sacrifice as belonging both to Christ and to the Church. Indeed, as far as the texts of the liturgy go, the Sacrifice of the Church receives the greatest emphasis: the idea presented there is that the Church, the Plebs Sancta gathered together here and now, offers Sacrifice to God. That is the clear teaching of the "Unde et memores" which of all parts of the Canon most clearly sets forth the meaning of the Mass. That this Sacrifice which the Church offers is the Sacrifice of Christ is, of course, presupposed, but it is never directly called that. This is not only the doctrine of the liturgies, but also of the Fathers, of the Pre-Tridentine theologians and of the Council of Trent itself. The Church offers Sacrifice by joining in the Sacrifice of Christ; His offering becomes her offering; the one eternal Sacrifice is made present by the act of consecration done by the ministry of the priest; the immolated Body of Christ and the blood shed for the remission of sin are presented again to the Father. This is done by an action that is the external sign of Christ's Sacrifice on the cross: it is Christ who performs the action, using the lips of the priest who represents the Church. In the Consecration something is given and dedicated to God, something material is transformed, ceasing to be what it was and becoming "an eternal gift to Thee." By this action the offering of Christ is present upon our altars to give glory to God and to draw the Church and her members into His sacrificial and redemptive action. His transitus, His Pascha, His Paschal mystery becomes ours; His Sacrifice, the Sacrifice of the Church.

By His death on the cross Christ concluded a covenant between God and His people which bound them to God and God to them: "The chalice of my Blood, of the new and eternal convenant." That covenant must be entered into anew and ratified daily; this is done through the Mass. By it we signify our intention of adhering anew to the covenant and the alliance, of making Christ's Passion our passion and His Sacrifice ours. It is not a mere recalling to mind of something that was done; it is an accepting of it here and now. By accepting this Sacrifice and sharing in it we accept Christ and proclaim our willingness to embrace the cross. This is the very heart of Christianity: "Christ also suffered for us leaving you an example that you should follow his steps"; "Let that mind be in you which was also in Christ Jesus."

We enter into this Sacrifice and make it our own, first of all, by offering for consecration something which represents us in a special way: we offer bread and wine, the products of man's hands and at the same time the great "supports of his weakness," the staple elements of food and nourishment in our Lord's time. In addition, the words which make His sacrificial action present are words spoken by those members of a community who have been set aside to speak them. So in a twofold way the Mass is the offering of the Church: she sets aside the gift which represents her and she offers it to God. Thus the Church is most intimately associated with Christ in offering Sacrifice to God; as He offered Himself, so she offers herself. This means specifically that the faithful, particularly those gathered here and now at this Mass, offer sacrifice to God. The priest is not their substitute but their spokesman, who acts both in "persona Christi" and in "persona Ecclesiae" and who is empowered to present this sacrifice to God as their own Sacrifice.

Nor is this all: the priest offers a Sacrifice which is completed by being eaten; Mass is not offered without someone, at least the priest who represents the ecclesia, who eats the bread and drinks the wine. By this sacrificial meal the Church is joined in fellowship with Christ and with the members of Christ. This fellowship involves of necessity a sharing in His Passion, Death and Resurrection. The Mass is thus a Sacrifice-banquet. By eating and drinking of the Sacrifice the Church affirms her intention of joining with Him, of making His Sacrifice her Sacrifice. It is a ratification on her part of the covenant made between God and His people. By the offering she had made and

49

thus ratified the Church is thereby consecrated and dedicated to God. She not only renews the Sacrifice sacramentally upon the altar but renews it in herself; daily she sacrifices and daily renews her sacrificial frame of mind. That is what we mean when we say that the Mass is the center and source of Christian life, because it is through the Mass that the Church daily chooses to travel the royal road of the cross that leads to victory and ultimately to transfiguration into the likeness of Christ. "For if we suffer with Him we shall be glorified with Him."

Every Mass, then, represents or contains not only the objective representation of Christ's redeeming work—the opus operatum as the theologians call it—but also a Godward movement, an offering, an opus operantis on the part of the Church. The Mass is, first of all, interior, but it expresses itself in some way outwardly. The more strikingly and emphatically that outward expression is made the better. We can see throughout the history of the Church, and in all the liturgies that have been created to express and contain the worship of the Church, a preoccupation with this external, outward expression. Some liturgies show it more than others, but all of them have worked into the very structure of the worship some declaration in word and act that the Sacrifice which the Church offers daily is the sacrificial return of the whole "plebs sancta Dei."[1]

Wednesday, December 1. At the beginning of this class I had some routine items to consider: the boys who wanted to go Saturday, December 4, to St. Ann's for another Mass; the announcement of a film on December 9; some explanation about marks. Another interruption was some questioning about some elements of the Mass that I had just celebrated for the community. After this we got to the second half of the mimeographed text which I distributed. We read through it and then briefly

1. Westminster, 1957, pp. 303–307.

made some references to the Mass text. The students had their missals for this class.

Thursday, December 2. This class, in retrospect, seemed to have lacked sufficient preparation on my part. I went over liturgy notes again and then to the missal. Instead of having students find elements in text, I did it and hence missed the boat on some better teaching and learning.

Monday, December 6. This class took a completely unexpected turn. At St. Ann's on Saturday, the students asked Fr. Gannon about bringing, or, rather, obtaining toys for the children at St. Ann's. This had been their own idea and they had brought it up to the student council where it had been approved. Father Gannon suggested that perhaps they could give a party for some of the children of the parish. The students present at St. Ann's responded favorably, and on Monday the class time was given over to planning the party for the 19th of December for children from 10–14 years of age, fifty altogether. The students themselves are organizing and planning the party; Fr. Richardson and I are providing some guidance, but none of the actual implementation.

Thursday, December 9. We had planned about a month previous to show a film at this time. *The Nightwatch,* a thirty-minute television film, produced by the National Council of Catholic Men, was shown this day. It deals with the problem of a priest attempting to rouse the social conscience of his parishioners, with little success. There was not enough time, unfortunately, after the class for discussion; but the general reaction was good.

Monday, December 13. This class was directed to a discussion of the film. I asked the students what were the key ideas that hit them from this film. The first answer helped the whole class. One student was struck by the priest and his unwillingness to awaken the people. From there we evolved the reasons, etc. One student took notes for me from what I wrote on the blackboard. They are inserted below.

(I should comment on the reactions of the students who went to St. Ann's on December 3. We tried to have new students attend. Of the twelve who came, nine had not been present previously. We discouraged some of the earlier visitors since we do not like to come in too large a group. This Mass had a considerably smaller crowd, since there were only two sisters as opposed to almost thirty the time before. We arrived early enough to stop over at the convent to say hello to Sr. Thomas Marie. She was out for the afternoon, but two other sisters spoke with us and also took the students in two groups to the housing projects where they had an opportunity to meet one or two families and discover what a low-income project looked like. It was the first time for all of them. At the Mass they had the same experience of community as before. One student, who had been there previously, said he preferred it with the smaller crowd. I directed one or two of our students to mix more deliberately with the teenagers of the parish. Attendance from the parish was still small, but the priests are continuing their efforts to get their teenagers to come. We did not stay as late this time because a parish meeting was going to take place after the Mass. Some of our students, on their own, returned to that neighborhood the following week to help in another parish in setting up scenery for a Christmas play. This happened because of a meeting at the Mass in St. Ann's with some other teenagers who were involved in the play and needed help.)

THE NIGHTWATCH

1. The Priest—unwilling to awaken the people because
   a) his lonely life
   b) his fear of responsibility
   c) his own doubts
   d) he did not want to be ignored
   e) "   "   "   "   "   " rejected
   f) he wanted to keep the status quo
2. The People
   a) hypocrisy
   b) false sense of values
   c) status quo
   d) self-centeredness
   e) smallness
   f) superficiality
   g) prejudice
3. Night Watchmen—protagonist conscience
4. Negro—neutral
5. The Bells
   a) influence of the Church
   b) decline of influence
      —not wanted
      —time signal

Theme
  Problems
  a) with people
  b) with the leader
    —how to say his message
    —how to accept it himself
    —how to work
    —how to work with the people as they are despite what he
     may feel

Wednesday, December 15. I had started this class on some points of the film discussion, but my recollections are that the chairman of the party at St. Ann's asked for time for the party and the period was given over mostly to continued planning. Now that I think it over again, I realize that the class was given over, not to the party, but to the students' impressions of their visit to the housing project. It was interesting to get their comments on the housing situation and their over-all view of poverty. The students were vocal and seemed rather interested. The idea behind this step was to prepare them for what they would come upon when they got into the parish on Sunday.

Thursday, December 16. This class was devoted exclusively to the party. The final arrangements were made on presents, money, transportation, entertainment, and some general advice from me on how to handle the situation.

Sunday, December 19. The students had spent Friday afternoon and evening, and Saturday afternoon, wrapping and cataloging presents. One student supervised the entire operation and handled it very well. They had collected and wrapped about 240 presents and had, in addition, about twenty large prizes to be raffled off, including two bikes, an excellent train set, two pairs of ice skates and some very large toys and a large doll. At approximately 12:30 P.M., Sunday, the students arrived at school, altogether about 40 students and four faculty members. They loaded the school's pickup truck and a student and myself drove it to the parish. When we arrived there, the others had unpacked the food they had brought, and the 16 new sweaters obtained from a manufacturer (gotten through one of the students), and had already made a schedule of the afternoon with one of the sisters there. They unloaded the toys, arranged them into piles for boys and girls (horsed around a little with a football), and received instruction from Sr. Thomas Marie on how to handle the children. She suggested that they try to stay with one or two all during the party and in that way get to know them as persons. She asked that they get the 65 children to cooperate so that there wouldn't be bedlam.

The schedule was as follows:

(1) Meet children and get them seated.

(2) Entertainment by four juniors with guitars.

(3) Entertainment by some of the children.

(4) Broken into groups for pantomime contest.

(5) Refreshments at the table, served by the boys, while children planned their pantomimes with one senior with each group.

(6) Pantomime contest with prizes to winning group.

(7) Santa Claus and raffle of big prizes.

(8) Christmas carols.

(9) Distribution of presents to all children.

(10) Dismissal with gifts of fruit and candy packages
(wrapped by family of one of the boys).

The boys then cleaned the hall and went home around 5:30
P.M. Some of them went over to another parish to watch a
Christmas show going on there. General reaction of boys, sisters,
and priests was enthusiastic. It seemed that the boys had gotten
through to the children and the children to the students.

Monday, December 20. Discussion of party. First thing that hit
some of them was that the children were not in rags. They also
thought that the children seemed contented with what they had.
The neighborhood was better than expected, although students
who visited project commented on that. They noticed the con-
trol the sisters had. At the party Sr. Thomas Marie had asked
that one of our students talk with a boy about 18 or 19 who was
visiting that day. She said he was one of her "boys." I sent one
of the seniors over to him, and he spoke in class about this young
man who had been a member of a gang, involved in gang wars,
with police, etc., and with whom sister had been able to work.
The students were interested in this report. Sister Thomas Marie
had also pointed out that one of the girls who won a bike was
one of four girls and the father earned $55.00 a week. They
noticed that children took home some of the food, and that they
were very polite.

The general reaction of faculty members present was one of
enthusiasm for the way in which the seniors planned and carried

off the entire day. One or two students at the party were less than concerned, but the general effort and over-all results were satisfactory. We felt that they were learning how to give to others.

Wednesday, December 22. This day was rather poorly handled. It was the last class before Christmas assembly. Frankly, I was overtired and, while prepared, not ready to teach in good fashion. I brought in a copy of the *National Catholic Reporter,* and *The Critic* with an article by Philip Scharper on the meaning of Christmas. It was rather somber reading, stressing the poverty in the world and the sentimentality attached to the Christchild. I asked for comments after the reading and got them. The students were negative towards the negative articles and I asked the students for their ideas on Christmas. Need more preparation.

Wednesday, January 5. This was the first class after vacation. I spoke with the class about my reaction to the parishioners in the parish where I vacationed. I had said the New Year's Eve Mass in Our Lady's Parish in Nassau, the Bahamas. It was a very moving experience for me and I tried to transmit the idea to the class. We also discussed sending thank-you notes for the party to certain people outside the school who assisted in the Christmas party. I mentioned to one student, who has been rather unresponsive, that I had thought of him in terms of surfing, which he enjoys very much. In view of my reading from Fr. Pierre Babin, I attempted to relate his natural enjoyment of surfing with any religious experiences he has had. It didn't work, but it gave me a lead for the next day.

Thursday, January 6. On this day I asked the same student about surfing. I explained that I wasn't being facetious or wasn't mocking him out. I asked him to explain to me why he liked surfing and what it required. He pointed out the following: experience, practice, balance, stamina, and, I added, nerve. All this was put on the blackboard. I asked him why he enjoyed this sport, or why any of the students enjoyed a basketball game, or watching a game. They arrived at the conclusion that these were above the ordinary things. It took a man outside himself. I generalized and we arrived at the idea that sports, music, shows, girls, all were human things that were necessary for a human, in one respect or another, to function as a complete human being. I asked the surfer, then, about ritual and vocabulary and he answered that they both were part of surfing. It was partly the challenge and also the experience he had had. He agreed that sometimes the prodding of his friends might also be a reason, or might help someone not too enthusiastic to try surfing. He stated that part of the enjoyment was doing it with others. I then asked the class to see if they could see any parallel between the items on the blackboard and the Eucharist. I pointed out to them that one of the keys to the answer might be in experience. Some of them saw the relationship in that if you experienced Eucharist you might be willing to try again. (The surfer said previously that you practiced in order to experience more fully and to get you ready for the bigger waves; you didn't start at the top. You needed practice in order to get the experience which would make you want to come back. He had the idea he really sensed the experience of surfing and would try to recapture or get any experiences possible because of what he has already done.) I asked the surfer if he could remember any experiences of Eucharist. The only one that came to mind was first communion, and then after a while he mentioned the recent senior closed retreat. I asked him what he felt then. He mentioned being closer to Christ and to his classmates. Some other students mentioned experiences of Eucharist which were memorable. I then asked them to consider the element of practice in surfing as related to the Eucharist. Some saw the point, but others were just beginning to get the idea when the period ended. I asked them to think about the question: What is the practice demanded in Eucharist? It will be continued next week.

Monday, January 10. We went directly into the question of what is the practice the Eucharist demands. (There were a few brief comments on an hour-and-a-half television show on surfing the previous night which was spectacular in terms of beauty and excitement.) I asked the students what was involved in practice for the Eucharist and they gave the following: remind yourself of what you are doing—this was clarified in terms of faith in what the priest was doing and God was doing. One student suggested preparation for the Eucharist but was a little vague on what he meant by that. Another suggested that one had to put into effect what he did in Eucharist so that it would become real. Another said that you had to extend yourself. I asked them after we had received all these answers whether the problem of remind-yourself and faith needed more clarification. I asked them what else was the object of faith after the priest and God. Finally, after many answers, one student thought of his fellow man. I didn't pursue this idea since I don't think we are ready yet to explore it, although I feel it must be included. One student pointed out that we must renew our sense of community and that we are a group, not just individuals. I then asked them what it meant to be a priestly people. Some hesitated at the term; I read them two passages from St. Peter's first epistle and they began to see their role in worship. I then went on to ask them which demanded more—Eucharist or surfing. The first answer was Eucharist since it was *abstract* (an interesting answer in view of community worship—it indicates how far we must go). I asked them what happens when they get involved in extracurricular activities such as the basketball team, the newspaper. They answered that it demanded time and effort. I asked them what happens when you get involved in Eucharist and they answered that it demanded that you get involved with others and that that is not always easy. One student said that what you get out of Eucharist is not proportional to what you get out of surfing, a rather interesting observation. Another student answered that you grow into Eucharist as you get older.

Wednesday, January 12. I had hoped this day to have the class open up on the topics of priestly people, community, and response to the Eucharist. I floundered in the beginning but finally asked the question about what we had learned from the discussion

60

on liturgy that was new or perhaps what insight they had had into what they knew already. This was a difficult question. The answer I received was interesting—we don't understand liturgy yet, i.e., we realize how little we know now. Another student pointed out that he had insight into the idea of worship as community. Another one said that liturgy and community cannot be separated. In discussion on why this is not obvious to more people, one student said he had the idea in general that the liturgy was the priest's show. (This was not meant critically, but as an observation of how the priest and people are together.) I realized I would have difficulty getting to the heart of the matter so I then decided to ask them which prayer in the Mass was the most meaningful for them; rather, I said which prayer in the canon. The answers were interesting and indicative. Several said the remembrance of the living or the dead, another the *Nobis quoque peccatoribus,* another the *Per ipsum,* two said the words of consecration, and three or four others the *Unde et memores.*[1] I pointed out to them that the prayers they thought most important illustrated their attitude towards what they were doing. One student said that we tend to worship by ourselves, we are not overly conscious of community worship. I then asked why we go to Mass, and then switched to would they go if it were optional here. My question finally came out as how many would like to have Mass less frequently. About 80 per cent agreed to

1. The phrases in Latin were known to the students. In terms of the English canon, these are the references: *Nobis quoque peccatoribus*—"For ourselves, too, we ask a place with your apostles and martyrs . . ."; *Per ipsum*—"Through him, in him, with him . . ."; *Unde et memores*—"So now, Lord, we celebrate the memory of Christ, your Son."

that.[1] I asked then why not go to Church just for a Bible service or just to be present. Why Mass? They didn't seem to get the point. One student said it was the center of his life, although we didn't have time to spell it out. Another said it was not the center of his life at all and he could be good without it. The student who spoke first recounted that it gave him union with Christ. Another said he went because Christ instituted the Mass at Calvary. I qualified that with the idea that the Last Supper was also involved. The period ended.

Thursday, January 13. I asked this class to consider two questions which I placed on the blackboard. On one side of the board I wrote, "What was Christ's purpose in establishing the Eucharist?" On the other, "Why do we go to Mass?" I added that the two should have a strong relationship, but I didn't expect it necessarily. I received four answers to the first question:

(1) aid to man in sharing divine life;
(2) continue work of redemption in such a way that man might join in Christ's paschal mystery;
(3) to provide a way of worship;
(4) to provide a source of common life.

I then asked why answers 2, 3, and 4 were included in the

1. The objections to daily Mass may seem somewhat surprising to readers who expect minor seminarians to have a well-developed spirituality, one with no unresolved problems, at the age of seventeen or eighteen. Questions on religious practices are common enough in today's Church. Questions about Mass attendance do not indicate a lack of respect for the Mass, but may indicate that the approach to Mass today may have to take into account different levels of appreciation and understanding, especially for adolescents.

first. I turned to one student and asked him what it meant to share divine life. He asked me what that was. I asked him if he had it at any time. He wasn't sure. I asked him when he received it, and another student in the back of the room inadvertently said at holy communion. I asked this last student about grace, sanctifying grace, and spelled out the idea of a gift which makes us holy. What were the signs of life, of grace? I mentioned Sr. Thomas Marie as sharing in life, as life being an outgoing thing (I should have gotten this from the students), and I displayed for them the idea of Inferno illustrated by contemporary themes from *Life* magazine. We were making some progress towards the idea of life at the end of the period. I asked what in the Gospel was the sign of divine life. I finally got the answer Christ.

Monday, January 17. I put the reasons for Christ's institution of the Mass on the blackboard and then asked them for the reasons for our going to Mass. They gave them as follows (the wording is mine, and they are not given in the order of importance):

(1) obligation (fear)
(2) habit
(3) convenience in acknowledging God
(4) human respect (community pressure)
(5) refuge from tension
(6) reward
(7) desire to worship
(8) self-gratification

(9) petition

(10) for social effects of community

We then proceeded to analyze these. Again I was at fault in that I did most of the analysis.

Wednesday, January 19. For this class I had the reasons reproduced and given to the class in order to save time writing on the blackboard. We discussed the relationship between the two sets of reasons. I recollect that the students commented on the lack of a sense of worship in the reasons we go to Mass. It became evident that we all had much to learn and much to rethink on the meaning of Eucharist.

Thursday, January 20. On this day I asked the students to have their copies of the Constitution on the Liturgy. I read from it and then asked for their comments and explanations on sections applying directly to the Eucharist. It summed up for them our work on the question of the meaning of Eucharist.

Wednesday, January 26. Their final examination is reproduced below. *The final examination results indicated a general understanding of the problem of community and liturgy on the part of the students.* Much emphasis was given by the students to the need for a better awareness on their own part of community.

FINAL EXAMINATION

Answer all questions on the answer paper which will be provided for you. Please return the question paper at the end of the examination.

(1) The following statement was made at the Twenty-Fifth North American Liturgical Week in 1964. Comment on it in the light of our classroom discussion relative to community and liturgy.

"The Christian, like the faith and love which are his life, is defined by his relation to God and to the Christian community. His most distinctively Christian activity, then, will be the community's worship—that is, the activity by which the community as a community expresses its relation to God, the members by that very act simultaneously expressing their relation to one another.

"Unless we want to lead lives of fraternal love, it makes no sense to be a Christian—since love of and in the community of the Church is the substance of the Christian life. Unless we want to forge others and ourselves into a community of Christian love, it makes no sense to promote participation, or involvement, in the liturgy—since that is the meaning of the Christian community's worship."

(2) In the light of our classroom discussions and your own reflection, comment on what you feel is significant in the following passages from the Constitution on the Liturgy.

(a) "At the Last Supper, on the night when he was betrayed, our Saviour instituted the Eucharistic Sacrifice of his body and blood. He did this in order to perpetuate the sacrifice of the cross throughout the centuries until he should come again, and so to entrust to his beloved spouse, the Church, a memorial of his death and resurrection: a sacrament of love, a sign of unity, a bond of charity, a paschal banquet in which Christ is eaten, the mind is filled with grace, and a pledge of future glory is given to us."

(b) "The Church, therefore, earnestly desires that Christ's faithful, when present at this mystery of faith, should not be there as strangers or silent spectators; on the contrary, through a good understanding of the rites and prayers they should take part in the sacred action conscious of what they are doing, with devotion and full collaboration. They should be instructed by God's word and be nourished at the table of the Lord's body; they should give thanks to God; by offering the immaculate victim, not only through the hands of the priest, but also with him, they should learn also to offer themselves; through Christ the mediator, they should be drawn day by day into ever more perfect union with God and with each other, so that finally God may be all in all."

SECOND SEMESTER

Wednesday, February 2. By chance we had available for this class a short film, *The Neighbors,* produced by the National Film Board of Canada.[1] It was obtained for the Catholic Interracial Council of the school. It takes about ten minutes. The students liked it so much that they asked that I repeat it during the same period. Briefly it goes as follows: Two very similar men are sitting in their yards in front of identical homes (stage houses set in a real yard), reading identical papers, both with headlines dealing with war and peace. They are pleasant and helpful, sharing a light for their pipes. A small flower grows between them. It would appear to be right on the property line. They become possessive and their animosity grows into hate leading to destruction and death over the flower. At the end the words *Love Your Neighbor* are flashed on the screen in many languages. The students seemed very impressed by the film, but we did not have sufficient time to discuss it.

Thursday, February 3. Students were permitted to attend a special showing of the film *Othello.* I had not known about

1. This represents another common teaching situation—an on-the-spot situation that possibly can be used with a class, even though not originally scheduled. I had not ordered the film for the class; but, when I found out that it was available, I decided to use it since its theme fitted into our program.

this in advance, or far enough in advance, so I was caught off guard. Hence discussion of the film never materialized.

Monday, February 7. I asked their opinion today about how to handle *Pacem in Terris*,[1] explaining that I thought they should become involved in the encyclical. I asked for possible areas of concentration that might be studied. They gave me the following suggestions:

(1) admission of Red China to the U.N.
(2) communism and socialism
(3) Vietnam
(4) U.S. in the world
(5) disarmament
(6) poverty programs
(7) man's rights, e.g., apartheid
(8) Christian international responsibilities
(9) national sovereignty
(10) the U.N.

I then asked them how we could go about it. Some suggestions were:

(1) follow topics as they come up in the encyclical

1. This may seem to be an abrupt and inconclusive end to the section on the Eucharist and community, with no real transition to the new section. In retrospect I can see the lack of introduction. On the other hand, I realized that the students had gone far enough on the first topic in terms of their receptivity; further development, I feared, might prove boring. Also I began to understand that some material could not be totally absorbed. Age and wisdom would bring insight to the students. An opening to ideas with as much background as possible was what I felt I could accomplish.

(2) read the text in class

(3) seminar approach (following what they had done in third year).

I asked for possible speakers they might like to hear. It included poverty-program workers and clergymen concerned about Vietnam.

Sensing a stalemate in their response, I asked what the problems were facing the world in terms of peace. They gave the following:

(1) lack of trust

(2) communist threat to peace

(3) racial unrest

(4) lack of love in the most basic human relationships, moral disturbances

(5) unequal distribution of material goods

(6) national sovereignty

(7) economic greed

(8) nationalism

(9) ideological differences

(10) religious differences.

Wednesday, February 9. The senior class was involved in psychological testing for entrance into the college department of the seminary.

Thursday, February 10. I brought to the class a possible approach to the study of the encyclical. I suggested that we study the text carefully and then think of four possible topics, e.g., U.N., disarmament, human rights, economic inequalities (aid to other nations, poverty programs). After careful study, which might involve class time in the library, they would present a symposium to their parents. Surprisingly enough, most of the class reacted fairly well. Some worried about what they could say, how parents would react, but none seemed to reject the idea. It will be considered further by Fr. Richardson and myself, plus the rector and Fr. Ronald Barry, chairman of the religion department.

Saturday, February 12. Meeting with Fr. Ron Richardson on aims in teaching *Pacem in Terris.*[1]

Several questions came to mind at first:

Does the Christian have a relation to the world as a Christian?

Does the Christian have a relationship to the world by reason of his humanity?

Might not a student say we must think of Christianity in terms of personal sanctification?

Basically, what is the heart of the message we are trying to give or trying to share with the students? Is it real to them? Will it be meaningful? How meaningful can and should it be? What is the kerygma?

In analyzing *Pacem in Terris* we were conscious that Pope John is stressing the means in the natural order that exist for peace on earth. Hence what are we aiming for? A simply

1. Fr. Richardson and I met frequently during the year to discuss problems arising in both classes. Only on occasion did I write up these meetings. In rereading these notes, I can see where we wanted to arrive. Why I didn't in my own class will be evident from the notes. Yet I feel that the statement of aims at intervals helped me keep some perspective on the program.

natural soultion. Yet, John speaks of the role of the Christian witness in working with the natural order; he talks of the Christian requirement of love in having Christians work with all men, using the laws of God as understood by all men—laws which are reflected in man's nature, in order to secure a peaceful society.

We felt that we are trying to bring the students to see the need of man in the larger community. In the past semester we attempted to have them see the relationship between community and liturgy, between themselves as individual Christians and the necessary correlation with other Christians. We think the students are beginning to have an awareness of the problem, to see the existence of a bond between liturgy and the Christian community.

It was thought that the teacher should see how the student views a community, how he understands the world around him. There is the twofold element: the principles or themes the student needs to understand or to be exposed to, and the world in which the student is living and which is most real to him. How to bring these two into a workable focus is the problem.

Does the student see the encyclical and its problems as real? If not, is it also possible that it is the work of the teacher to open up to him these areas in such a way that he sees the relevance of the Christian message to the world in areas where Christian light is needed, e.g., race issues, human rights, peace, international cooperation, the concern of brother for brother.

Discussion will continue in the ensuing weeks.

Monday, February 14. I was prevented from attending class by my work with students going to the opera.

Wednesday, February 16. I gave an introduction to encyclicals, mentioning significant statements of Leo XIII, Pius XI, Pius XII, John XXIII. I then showed the students the outline given in our edition of *Pacem in Terris.* In discussing John's introduction, one student pointed out that much depended on a person's view of man, man's nature. He indicated that the view of man in Golding's *The Lord of the Flies* would differ from that of Pope John. We left off at that point.

Thursday, February 17. This class began with the idea which we had discussed the previous day: the nature of man. I said that Pope John took a somewhat optimistic view and asked could they bring to mind any societies or men that were effectively reasonable without being formally organized on a religious level, i.e., was it possible for man to follow order in his natural state. Some examples were the Roman Empire, Quakers, League of Nations (*sic*), Gandhi, Schweitzer (not necessarily valid in every respect), Switzerland, Athens, Buddhists. One student mentioned (after I had waited for it) the U.S. Constitution. I asked how the Constitution's view of man differed from that of Golding's in *The Lord of the Flies.* Somehow we arrived at the idea that the Constitution took a realistic view of human nature, i.e., took into account differences, problems, difficulties of men living together, and managed adequate checks and balances. In Golding's novel, you have the problem of inadequate controls over the deficiencies of human nature that can disrupt an inadequately ordered society. We pointed out the controls in the Constitution. Students offered examples of that. Going back to the commentary on *Pacem in Terris,* I pointed out that the Pope has taken a realistic view of man, as he is, not idealized.

I asked for examples of societies that took a different view of the nature of man. Rather I asked, first, for examples of societies that did not succeed. One student suggested Russia and I then asked why. We arrived at the idea that there is a different understanding of the nature of man involved there. The Russian society doesn't take into consideration the possible existence of different classes. African societies, today, were considered immature. In Nazi Germany, one student said, there were false goals, and a misunderstanding of the inequality of man, with the emphasis on the master race.

I then asked them what they thought were the rights of man according to the idea of their own human nature. They gave the following:

(1) to think as you please
(2) to freedom of speech
(3) to freedom to live
(4) to life itself
(5) to privacy
(6) to compete, to work
(7) to private property
(8) to disagree, to assemble, to associate
(9) to religion

Monday, February 21. I asked the class, after I had handed out a sheet listing the above rights, to consider the implications of these rights. They pointed out that rights involved duties, and responsibilities. A duty to respect the rights of others, and a responsibility in handling one's own rights. I asked for specific examples of how rights could be abused. They pointed out that private property could become a monopoly, e.g., in some areas of South America. Violations of right to work because of race, etc. An interesting situation arose when a student said he had been denied a job because the employer felt he had or wanted to hire a Negro because he was a Negro. This raised considerable discussion. One student said it was necessary for people to take extraordinary means to correct social abuses; another felt that you could not be just merely by being not unjust. Another student, in the same general area, said he felt that that approach would not substitute for internal change. He said that we should use firecrackers, not atomic bombs, in social change. Another student said you cannot or should not use lethal means to gain someone else's rights. In the class, somewhere before this discussion, a student said it was the obligation, from our own rights, to stand up for the rights of others. I pointed out the problem of the conflict of rights and how the Pope speaks of the need for order in society. I asked them how the discussion that day related to the liturgy, which included Paul's letter on love. One student said that he noticed the line that says love seeks out the truth and that he thought we should be concerned about men. In commenting on this idea the students pointed out that (1) we don't always know or have the truth, (2) truth might hurt us, (3) we overlook the truth.

For an assignment I asked them to list all the rights Pope

John talks about and then to develop some ideas on them for a short paper.

Wednesday, February 23. The discussion this day revolved around the Mass that this class will have on March 1.[1] It will mean that they will celebrate Mass with me during the fourth period of the morning. Then we will have lunch together while the remainder of the school is at the regular community Mass. I asked for their suggestions about what they would like in those areas of the liturgy where there can be variation. Some suggestions had to be turned down; others were referred to a committee of five who will present their ideas on Monday, February 28.

Some time at the end of the period was given over to the meaning of Lent.

Thursday, February 24. I was out of class, on an outing to the Metropolitan Opera House with a group of 38 students. The religion class had a study period.

1. Spring of that year saw the beginning of class Masses at the school. The original idea was tied in with the theme of Eucharist and community which the senior classes have been discussing. It was felt that the experience of the Eucharist in the small class group might help the students understand more easily what they had been discussing. The more direct participation, made possible by the small numbers, would help them see what they were involved in at the larger community Masses.

In practice this Mass has been most successful. It has become a regular practice of each class to celebrate Mass approximately once a month with the religion or homeroom teacher. The students themselves feel that the experience of the class Masses has helped them to understand the Eucharist, and they feel that they now bring more to the larger community Masses.

77

Monday, February 28. The committee chairman presented his findings. The students will recite the propers together; they have chosen four hymns; there will be an offertory procession; they have made their own suggestions for the prayer of the faithful; they will stand fairly close to the altar from the offertory on. The rest of the period was given over to Lent and its meaning, especially the significance of the 40 days and the meaning of the desert symbol in the Christian life.

Tuesday, March 1. Although this was not a class day for religion, we had the class Mass. It went smoothly and the students reacted well to having it by themselves. We ate lunch together, but there was no real time for discussion with about 35 students. The experience of eating together was good.

Wednesday, March 2. I asked the differences between Mass with themselves and with the community: greater sense of unity, no rush getting to lunch; no distractions from freshmen; spirit of Mass was greater; size was all right; one felt it was closer sense of unity than St. Ann's since it was their own class.

Position around the altar should be rectified and perhaps kiss of peace added among the students. We then went on to Lent again, I think, but I'm not sure since I didn't take any more notes.

Thursday, March 3. I reminded them of assignment first. Then we read paragraph 35 in *Pacem in Terris.*[1] I asked them to think

1. "(35) A political society is to be considered well ordered, beneficial and in keeping with human dignity if it is grounded on truth. As the

of it in practical terms. An important element seems to have been truth for the students—to understand it and to see how it is implemented. It is the problem of conflicting ideas on truth. To understand or examine, to explore its implications, to act upon it, these were the criteria that we ended up with. This led to problems, specific ones, in communities on Long Island, where there is racial discrimination. This class was not too successful since we didn't really come to grips with the core of the passage but skirted around in generalities. This was probably my fault since I had not thought it out sufficiently myself.

Monday, March 7. I started with a reminder about the assignment due on Thursday. I then read briefly from the morning paper about the Orthodox Church and its revival in contemporary Russian thought on a limited scale. I then proceeded to the lesson. (In each class we begin with a reading from the Gospel of John.) I asked them to think of the problems of the encyclical in terms of a particular community. Since we had been discussing

---

apostle Paul exhorts us: *Wherefore, put away lying and speak truth each one with his neighbor, because we are members of one another.* This indeed will be the outcome when reciprocal rights and duties are sincerely recognized.

"Furthermore, human society will be such as we have just described it, if the citizens, guided by justice, apply themselves seriously to respecting the rights of others and discharging their own duties; if they are moved by such fervor of charity as to make their own the needs of others, and share with others their own goods; if, finally, they everywhere work for a progressively closer fellowship in the world of spiritual values. Moreover, human society is realized in freedom, that is to say, by ways and means in keeping with the dignity of its citizens, who accept the responsibility of their actions precisely because they are by nature rational beings."

the questions of rights and duties, I asked them to think of themselves as a priest or lay leader in St. Ann's parish or in some similar situation. The problems they had to face were as follows:

(1) acceptance
(2) "love of neighbor"
(3) ethnic prejudices
(4) poverty
(5) size of problem
(6) self-respect
(7) education
(8) apathy
(9) crime
(10) family life
(11) unemployment

I then asked how they would approach this situation and what steps had to be taken. First was acceptance of the leader by the community; then social services from government which were outside the community; then acceptance of the people by the leader (we had various examples given by them on this matter); then I reminded them of what Sr. Thomas Marie had told them last semester and they then thought of self-help. One student pointed out that the leader should not treat the people as children, helping them; rather the people should begin to help themselves. Another student mentioned cooperation with surrounding communities. This led to a discussion of the value of ghettos, in terms of building strength before assimilation, etc. I asked them about possible solutions.

Here were some: need a leader within and with other communities; knowledge (this involved questioning about the type of knowledge) and then commitment. At the end of this period, I asked them if they preferred this approach to the encyclical and they seemed more satisfied with it than with an abstract reading of the text.

Wednesday, March 9. I played a tape on *Pacem in Terris* which we obtained from the Center for Democratic Studies in Santa Barbara, California. It runs an hour and the discussion is led by John Cogley. One of the other participants is Robert Hutchins. The tape lasted for one hour and will take up another class period.

Thursday, March 10. I played the other part of the tape. General reaction of the students was good, especially in terms of hearing laymen and non-Catholics discussing the encyclical. Unfortunately, I should have scheduled it when I had time for more discussion. Our next class is the following Monday which is too far away from the sound of the tape. The general approach of the tape is directed more to international aspects and we have been on the personal aspects at present.

I collected their essays on the rights of man—generally good. They are becoming more conscious of the difficulty involved in conflict of rights: some see a solution in a willingness to help others; some still insist on rights being protected, but do not see how some rights must be shared or modified for the common good.

Monday, March 14. I was not prepared for this class and told the students so. I asked them if there were any topics they wanted to discuss. The first topic raised was the question of conflict of rights. We discussed the question of inalienable rights, absolute rights, rights that must be subordinated to the common good, e.g., traffic laws, property for schools and roads, etc. Then the question of pacifism came up: was it moral to be a conscientious objector? The discussion became quite lively and had some odd turns to it. One student said you had to obey the government if the majority followed it. Students quickly opposed that. Much difficulty arose over the morality of pacifism. One student had a copy of *The Catholic Worker.* We did not resolve the problem of pacifism, but it was made clearer that an individual had a right to follow his own conscience.

Wednesday, March 16. On this day I asked them to review back about two weeks for the cost of involvement in a community. They said a leader must be willing to give time, money, loss of friend's support, reputation, life, private life and ideas. One student pointed out the problem of N.Y.C. Housing Commissioner Moerdler, whose in-law's property was being investigated for housing violations.

We then proceeded to the relation of the individual and the state. What was the authority of the state? One student said it came from the people, another from God. I asked if a state could be overthrown: one student said no just government could rightfully be overthrown by violence; when questioned about a just government, he said it was one that protected rights of individuals. A conflict arises when a person makes a judgment that rights are not being respected. Somewhere in this class we pointed out that some people are not ready for some types of government and that we can't judge all governments by our own.

Thursday, March 17. Feast of St. Patrick; school holiday.

Monday, March 21. After reading of St. John's Gospel, briefly discussing the class Mass for next week, and introducing the students to an essay contest sponsored by the Long Island Catholic Interracial Council, the time for encyclical amounted to about fifteen minutes, so I switched to a discussion of the TV show "Open End" which had appeared the previous evening. I discovered all the students had missed it,[1] so I gave a quick rundown. It was on the *aggiornamento* in the religious communities of women.

Wednesday, March 22. Class president presented program for class Mass for next week (see below). Controversy started over the music selected. I decided to allow discussion and it came. Some felt it was too gimmicky, novel; others favored it in terms of their own cultural level. It got rather personal. I suggested that plans for a community Mass should show some sense of community. Two views became evident: those who were against

1. Here is an example of projecting one's own interest on students. I was interested in the question of the updating of religious life and thought the students had "missed" something. Perhaps they were not interested. Religion teachers can begin to see the world too professionally; we can't presume everything that interests us interests our students.

radical change; those who favored them. Some, of course, were neutral, but not too many. It was a healthy discussion and I'm glad it came out in the open. Students were to vote the next day. I pointed out the role of negotiation stressed in *Pacem in Terris* and indicated that they had just received a practical lesson. Music included "When the Saints Come Marching In," "Turn, Turn, Turn," "We Shall Overcome," and a Somerville Psalm. (One student said he would never sing "We Shall Overcome.")

MASS PROGRAM

1. Entrance hymn: "God Called Us All."
   a) Prayers at the foot of the altar—Zuchelli.
2. Introit and subsequent propers:
   a) Led by Pisarski.
   b) Epistle read by Pisarski.
3. Gospel:
   a) Read by Fr. Murphy.
4. Stirring Homily:
   a) Fr. Murphy.
5. Offertory:
   a) Prayer of the faithful's intentions to be said by students who have intentions. All intentions are included here.
   b) Begin hymn "Turn, Turn, Turn."
   c) Place host in ciborium or paten.
   d) After placing host in the ciborium, gather around the altar.
   e) The wine and water are to be taken care of by Wood and Gulla.
6. Sanctus:
   a) Recited by the community.
7. Great "Amen" After Doxology:
   a) Sung (like good Protestants) to the melody in "Lilies of the Field."

8. Agnus Dei:
   a) At the conclusion of the Agnus Dei we will have the kiss of peace in the form of a double-clasp handshake.
9. Communion:
   a) Hymn "Taste and See."
   b) Verse to be recited by the community.
10. Conclusion:
   a) Hymn "We Shall Overcome."

Thursday, March 24. I discovered that the Mass for next week cannot be held because of scheduling difficulties. Students were disappointed. Interestingly enough, one of the students who has little external enthusiasm had helped set up this program for next week and really wanted it. It will come after Easter. I could not get to this class today because of the showing of the film *Julius Caesar* to the sophomore English classes I teach. Also it was impossible to switch the class to the morning since the other teachers couldn't adjust their teaching schedules.

Saturday, March 26. Father Richardson and I met to discuss the course again. We spent considerable time trying to come to grips with what we are attempting to do in this section of the course. We both have some dissatisfaction with the over-all picture in our classes. Practically, however, we have decided to see what we can do after the Easter vacation to have the students tie in their reading with some research on their own and present some type of panel for the two classes and perhaps an even wider audience.

Monday, March 28. I attempted to get back to the text this period. We started with the idea of the common good. I asked them what elements had to be considered in terms of the common good and they gave the following:

(1) acceptance of differences
(2) laws
(3) food and shelter
(4) education
(5) recreation
(6) employment
(7) freedom of religion
(8) insurance
(9) cultural programs

I asked them then where the tension arose in specific cases between groups or between the individual and the group. Some areas pointed out were in education, employment. I asked them if they saw or remembered any specific case in their own experience where groups were at odds over differences in some area. They did not remember their dispute the week before over music for their Mass. I think it took the entire period to cover the above. Unfortunately, I did not take careful notes this period. Also the school newspaper was distributed at about ten minutes before the end of the period.

Wednesday, March 30. I started this period off with reading from the text where Pope John mentions the items necessary for the common good. It included areas the students had not considered, but generally they were close. (I would rather have them come to the conclusions or information on their own and then seek the text. It makes the text, difficult as an encyclical can seem, more real since it confirms or explains what they have discussed. I should follow up this method more carefully.) We then proceeded to the type of government that would be most suitable throughout the world for peace in a particular situation. I specified it in terms of what would be needed in emerging nations. The first suggestion was for dictatorship, which most students agreed to. It was interesting. The dictator should be honest, powerful, and have the support of the people. Examples of dictators who have helped emerging nations or nations of political instability to achieve some degree of stability were given as Tshombe, Mao, MacArthur (Japan), De Gaulle, Sukarno. What was necessary in dictatorship also was: security for the common good, open news media, delegation of authority. No one considered the question of courts. Ultimately, someone mentioned rights of the individual. In all this I did not have time to let any aspects of the question evolve more carefully or in greater depth. It involves a judgment on other nations, a certain naïveté, and yet a certain awareness of world conditions. What was lacking was an understanding of the device of government and its operation. I had them read what the Pope said about adjusting to historical conditions and the role of the three-part system, legislative, judicial, executive.

Thursday, April 1. This class got lost along the way. I, along with all religion teachers, had been asked to prepare for the Bible service to be held on Friday. I mentioned the service and some groans were evidenced. I let the students talk about the question of Bible services, First Friday, and popular devotions.

Their remarks revealed quite a bit. Bible services were not to their liking, in general.[1] They complained that they were held too frequently, too soon (two hours) after Mass; the books were used too much, not enough imagination. Since the reason for First Friday was a thing of the past in terms of our present Eucharistic practice, did we have to follow it? This also raised other questions. As it turned out, the period went by quickly. At the conclusion of their questioning and discussion, I decided to return to the encyclical and I read to them from the Declaration of Independence on the right and duty of overthrowing an unjust government. It raised a few questions.

Next week, Holy Week, I would like to spend the two class periods on the liturgy, hopefully.

Monday, April 4 (Holy Week).[2] I started by asking the students to consider the meaning of Holy Week in terms of the community here at school, at Manhasset (white upper-class surburban), at Lakeview (Negro surburban ghetto), at St. Ann's, in Vietnam. This threw them a little. A few mentioned how difficult it would be for a person in St. Ann's to appreciate Holy Week,

1. The question of allowing students to object to school policy is a delicate one. Simply to allow complaining has little educational or practical value; to listen to students' thinking and reactions can be of value if it does not mean endorsement of what they say, but provides an opportunity to explore problems or to help them see a situation more clearly.

2. The feasts of Easter and Christmas are normal interruptions in a catechetical program. They cannot be ignored, and yet they sometimes interrupt the program at hand since they cannot always be integrated into the subject matter under discussion.

but later they gave other answers, after they had rethought the matter. I then asked them what was the present meaning of Holy Week. Some said that it was more or less a historical event which we reconsidered. I then asked what meaning Holy Week had for themselves. The first answer was renewal. We spent a lot of time trying to define, or to specify, renewal. Returning to the situation at St. Ann's, I asked how Holy Week would be meaningful there. One mentioned that the parishioners might be bitter there because they know what the white people are preaching on those days and they see how they are treated. Another said they would have a greater idea of suffering. It could also give, another student said, real hope not for physical delivery, but for the meaning of life. One hope would come from realistic insight into the value of religion. I brought them back to the topic of ourselves here and renewal. One student said we were to go through the passover with Christ. Another student thought that was too gimmicky. We go through the motions to renew ourselves, to become holy (but we get over it after a couple of hours, according to one student). Another said the Easter vigil brought us to new life. Another said the community should try harder. I asked them what was happening, in one sense, and finally asked them to consider the idea of a new consciousness of ourselves. We did not arrive at the idea of the sacramental presence, life-giving element, of Christ in these days. Perhaps that will come tomorrow.

Wednesday, April 6. In this class I asked the students to think about the relationship of Holy Week in their own parish and the community in which the parish was located. This was extremely difficult for them, and I asked again in terms of St. Raymond's parish. I asked what was the relationship between the services in St. Raymond's and the community of Lynbrook and East Rockaway. The first and only response to that was that the people around the church would know something was happening because of the extra policemen needed to direct traffic. Failing on that score, I decided to rephrase. I asked what would be the ideas that the people in the parish would have at Mass, what would they be looking for in the Holy Week services. One student came up with the idea that the people would be looking for their own needs, what the services would give them and them alone. In other words, the services were just for themselves. I then asked what was the other possibility: the answer was that Holy Week would give the parishioner an idea of what they should be doing in relation to others; that the parishioners should be more Christian, more conscious of their fellow men.

They seemed to have gotten the idea on that point. As I began to sum up the ideas, a new problem arose from one of the students. It revolved around the presence of Christ in the Church (in a sacramental form) and the meaning of the sacramental sacrifice in the Mass. One student had difficulty regarding the lack of the presence of Christ sacramentally after the Good Friday services. Also the idea of the lack of the presence of Christ on the altar on Good Friday until the Blessed Sacrament is brought from the repository. One student, fortunately, brought up the idea of the presence of Christ in each person and the idea that where two or three are gathered in his name, he is present.

This answer was not to indicate this presence as a sacramental one, but to bring up the idea that Christ was not absent totally, if not present sacramentally.

More difficulties arose on the idea of Christ dying in the Mass each time the Eucharist is celebrated. We had great difficulty in trying to explain or develop the idea of the Risen Christ offering worship to his Father, that the Mass is a making-present of the paschal mystery. I gave several books to the one student most upset about this idea. I hope we'll be able to spend some time on this matter before continuing with *Pacem in Terris*.

Monday, April 18. After collecting the essays for the Catholic Interracial Contest, I asked this class about going to see the film *The Gospel According to St. Matthew.* They were all in favor. Next we discussed Holy Week but it brought little in the way of discussion. There was some comment about the new translation, etc., but I let it drop. Presumably, a week after an event is too long after for discussion, especially if there was no major reflection.

I then proceeded into another introduction on the meaning of the Mass, starting with the idea of the relationship of God and Adam and then the new relationship of God and man in Christ. This included the idea also of baptism and Eucharist as sacraments of initiation.

Wednesday, April 20. On this day we continued the question of the Mass,[1] on the topics of the sacramental presence and the mean-

1. The return to a discussion on the Eucharist this semester was not

ing of sacrifice, using as the basic text *Sacraments of Initiation* by William O'Shea. From later reports, it seemed to have satisfied or cleared up a good number of the difficulties experienced earlier in understanding this topic.

My original outline for the class went as follows:

Adam — to Christ by way of baptism and Eucharist. Take idea of sacrifice and supper
Key ideas: Sacrifice is made present so that we can partake interiorly and exteriorly in Christ's act of obedience:
1. more perfect contact;
2. continual contact so that we become perfectly assimilated;
3. page 95, *Sacraments of Initiation,* sacrifice in another form;
4. different presence of Christ;
5. no physical immolation in the Mass—p. 96, O'Shea;
6. page 99, O'Shea.

Thursday, April 21. On this day I read them a letter from a former parishioner of mine who is stationed in Vietnam. He asked for questions from the class, and some students volunteered to give them to me on Friday. Then we began a discussion on an article in *Newsweek* which told of a priest who had married and presented his ideas to the press on marriage and the priesthood. It included comments from other writers on the subject. This lead to a discussion on the meaning of celibacy and the question of personality development. It was a rather interesting class; I

---

planned, but the discussion raised by Holy Week seemed to make it imperative to bring the matter up again, at least briefly.

It may also seem that there was a great deal of discussion on the Mass, with some neglect of other elements of the liturgy. I think this neglect was consciously made.

chose to discuss the matter since I knew that almost ten students received the magazine at home and I felt it would be wise to have them hear a discussion in the religion class rather than have them give an unguided treatment of the topic in a bull session.

Monday, April 25. I decided to get back to *Pacem in Terris.*[1] I think the idea of the symposium of the students on specified topics will have to be dropped because of a lack of time now and lack of organization. Some time will have to be given to St. John's Gospel and the last marking period would be best.

In this class I started by introducing the theme of the relationship between two states. I asked two students to represent heads of states and give me the problems they would see in relationship to their neighboring country. The following problems were given:

(1) border disputes
(2) armaments – lack of trust
(3) ideologies
(4) economic differences
(5) population problems
(6) race-culture-language differences
(7) leadership conflicts.

In giving these difficulties, the class provided examples from the present world. When asked what would be the key to solving

1. One of the major problems concerns the over-all plan. In the day-to-day discussion approach, there is a possible loss of view. I felt this loss rather strongly during the year. The first page of the notes was a constant reminder to me of what we wanted to do and what had happened.

these difficulties, the students provided two solutions—one was communication between nations, e.g., cultural exchange programs such as we have with U.S.S.R.; the other was the acceptance of the differences.

At this point we ran into some disagreements; the general idea was that we could or should not consider ourselves superior to other people. The first comment, however, was that "we're better than they are," e.g., African nations, the Far East. This was seconded by another student. Several objections were raised. This was showing a condescending attitude towards others, etc. I read them the following from the encyclical: "First among the rules governing the relations between states is that of truth. This calls, above all, for the elimination of every trace of racism, and the consequent recognition of the principle that all states are by nature equal in dignity." We began to run into more trouble. One student thought that almost impossible, too idealistic. Kenya does not have the dignity of Luxembourg, no background, etc. Another answer was that all men are created equal, even though with different talents, and so are states. Response: shouldn't be treated as equals, etc.

I asked them if we don't accept them as equals, what alternatives were there? I then read the remainder of paragraph 86 in the encyclical. One student thought the Pope was naïve. We got into the problem, which I didn't want at this point, of our relationship to the Dominican Republic insofar as we may have felt it necessary to interfere in her internal affairs because of our own sense of government. The class ended on this rather disputed point.

Wednesday, April 27. In this class we continued in the same general direction, but continuing further into the text. I reviewed first the material of the last class, stressing that I wanted them to see the principles underneath; however, it is important to give the principles life by working from some current examples. Working from paragraph 92, which states, in part, "political communities have the right to existence, to self-development, and to the means necessary for this," I asked them to consider this principle in terms of Red China. This provoked considerable discussion, which I asked them to conclude by reading the next paragraph, which treats and adds a possible approach to the problem by suggesting a type of negotiation. We did not resolve anything, but I think we explored some good areas.

Thursday, April 28. I mentioned at the beginning of the class that we probably would not be able to have the symposium because of a lack of time now. I also mentioned the coming religious art exhibit to be held here. Then I suggested we would skim through the encyclical in order to have some time for St. John's Gospel during the next marking period. We then reviewed the next few areas in the encyclical. I had a chart brought in from the library, while they were reading the section on disarmament, which showed the percentage of our national budget that goes for defense, i.e., sixty billion out of one hundred twelve billion, with approximately only three billion for education. This provoked considerable discussion, as did the section in the encyclical on disarmament, but the period ran out.

Monday, May 2. During this week we were having an exhibit of religious art and also the students were to see the film *The Gospel According to St. Matthew.* At the beginning of the period I had a review of the film read by one of the students. Then there followed an introduction to the art show by displaying some of the prints that would be on exhibit.

Wednesday, May 4. The class visited the art show; several teachers were present to answer questions and explain some of the many works on display.

Thursday, May 5. In the morning the entire high school went to the film. In the afternoon every section had a religion class. In the 4B section the following comments were made:

The first area discussed was that of the technique used by the director. The students hit on close-ups, music, silence, lack of color, understating in terms of characters and events. In terms of content, they discussed Christ as a powerful leader. They liked John the Baptist and the apostles. There was a great deal of discussion on the question of Christ, also on the Last Supper. For insights received they added the idea of Christ as a revolutionary and an angry young man. In general the film was provocatively received, if not always liked.

Monday, May 9. In this class I distributed two dittoed items. The first was a reprint of an editorial in *Maryknoll* magazine dealing with our affluent society and the defense budget. It provoked considerable comment pro and con. Students picked off weaknesses in the argument, but I feel some of them did that to avoid the central issue in the editorial, that America was draining her wealth in armaments instead of attempting the very difficult task of channeling her wealth to good. The editorial did not provide answers, but it did open and close some more doors. Some students seem to have taken it as an unrealistic proposal or criticism of America. Others saw the point in some fashion or other. It is reproduced below.

I then distributed the answers from the serviceman in Vietnam in response to their questioning. They are not profound but they did help the students to have a sense of closeness to the situation which is troubling them.

EDITORIAL: THE INSIDIOUS ANEMIA OF GROWTH

THERE is something wrong with a society that puts its major efforts in creating the power of death. It is easy for such a society to become blinded to its own disintegration.

The Aztecs were a great warrior nation. Every male had to serve in the army. War was made merely to keep the army in practice. Yet a few hundred Spanish soldiers were able to destroy the Aztec empire.

The Greeks also fought wars for war's sake. Greece was a nation of citizen soldiers. It was the preoccupation with war that destroyed the tremendous intellectual life that had developed in Greece and led to that country's eclipse.

History is full of examples of nations which lost influence and power because of overconcern with military stature. In their desire to build offensive strength, they undermined themselves at home. It did not take an enemy to destroy them. They ruined themselves. There is a lesson in history for the United States.

97

America's productive and inventive power has become myopic. It has been marshalled to create instruments of war with the result that American society has been undermined and its people do not know it. The gross national product is up, unemployment is down, and citizens have a personal prosperity that is unequalled in history. But this good life comes from defense spending.

Almost 70 per cent of America's technical researchers are employed by the military. Even our universities, formerly the realm of pure science and research, have fallen under the spell. University budgets today depend heavily on federal funds. At California Institute of Technology, 83.5 per cent of its budget is government money; Princeton, 75.3 per cent; Massachusetts Institute of Technology, 81.8 per cent.

The result has been that outside of military technology American technology is like a clock that is running down. Our merchant marine is at a low ebb, ships are old and not being replaced, vessels like the America are sold to foreign flags. Our railroad industry is antiquated—old trains, disappearing lines. Sixty per cent of the typewriters sold in the United States are imported. The United States has the oldest stock of metal working machinery of any industrial nation in the world. In 1963, 64 per cent of American machine tools were ten years old or older, compared with 50 per cent in the Soviet Union.

Once the United States was the Mecca for industrialists; people came to this country to learn how to do things. Today if one wants to learn how to design and operate high-speed railroads, he goes to Japan. If he wants to study the best methods for desalinization of water, he goes to England. If he wishes to learn the most modern and productive ways to fish, the Soviet Union has the answer.

Other nations have built up their military strength but not at the complete expense of national development. Germany and Japan are examples of nations that have become industrial giants since the end of World War II. In Germany 85 cents out of every research dollar is private with only 15 cents going to the military. In Japan the same figure applies. But in the United States the major portion of research and creativity is controlled by the military and space programs—both of which are unproductive.

In a speech before the United Nations Economic and Social Council U Thant, the Secretary General, pointed out that $120,000 million were being spent each year on arms. He then went on to say, "How much more could be achieved for the benefit of the whole world if even a part of these vast efforts could be redirected from producing the instruments of death to producing the instruments of growth and work and life! Roads and dams, water and fertilizer, steel and machines, houses and cities, skills and welfare—all these could provide an economic stimulus equal to that of arms production, all could therefore be as simply and as easily afforded by the richer States."

America is drifting towards depletion and disaster. Its people are blinded by their prosperity. A nation that drains its wealth into unproductive channels falls into deterioration. The great northeastern blackout was a warning that the whole nation can be plunged into darkness unless we find some way to end the arms race. It is not an easy problem with China and Russia threatening security. But man's inventive genius must find an alternative to war.

Wednesday, May 11. I started the section on "Pastoral Exhortations" from the encylical. This day and the next were given to more lecture since I felt we had to finish the material. I think my mistake here was not to receive the answers from the students, as I had done before. It would have worked and been more effective on both days and would have kept me out of the picture more.

Thursday, May 12. Concluded as stated above.

Monday, May 16. I was sick, so the class was given a study period by the substitute teacher.

Wednesday, May 18. I will be with my sophomore homeroom for the day, so that there will be no class in religion for the seniors.

Thursday, May 19. Ascension Thursday; school holiday.

Monday, May 23. I made some references to the coming U.N. trip.[1] Copy of the schedule was given to them the next day. During this period I started St. John's Gospel with a brief introduction. Unfortunately, with the U.N. trip coming, it was hard to go anywhere with St. John. I *talked* too much about John.

Wednesday, May 25. United Nations trip. The schedule for the day was as follows:

8:00 A.M.	Mass in chapel for students who could be there at that time.
9:00 A.M.	Left by bus ($1.00 round trip).
10:30 A.M.	Arrived at U.N., met by Miss Celesta Petro, a staff member of the U.N. who volunteered to arrange the program for the day.
10:45 A.M.	Regular tour of the U.N. (.50 each).
12:00 noon	Short time at meditation room, book shop.
12:30 P.M.	Briefing at the Protestant Center by staff member of the Center.
1:00 P.M.	Luncheon at cafeteria in Protestant Center. Approxi-

1. The trip to the U.N. had been discussed in September before classes started. Preparations were made several months in advance of the actual May date, especially in terms of finding a suitable date. We had hoped to go during the time of the General Assembly, but it could not be worked out.

mately twenty staff members of the U.N., workers with Miss Petro, agreed to have lunch with the students. Included members from Eastern bloc.

2:00 P.M.   To Holy Family Church, Catholic parish of U.N. Addressed by Monsignor Flynn, pastor of Holy Family; Miss Margaret Schaeffer, N.C.W.C. representative at U.N.; Fr. DeFillippo, secretary to representative of Holy See to U.N. Also present—Fr. Morley, representative of Catholic Press to U.N., and also present: representative of International Catholic Relief to U.N.

3:15 P.M.   Panel answered questions directed to them by students.

4:15 P.M.   Visit to Pacem in Terris Library at Holy Family Church.

4:30 P.M.   Return by bus to school.

General consensus was that the trip was an extremely valuable experience. Students were generally enthusiastic, attentive. Program was well planned by Miss Petro, although we had to drop two items because of lack of time.

Thursday, May 26. I opened the class by giving them some background on the trip to the U.N., i.e., some more information on the people involved. What seemed to have impressed them very much was the fact that many important people were willing to give time to them. In one or two cases, students could not understand why they were subject to that much attention. I tried to point out to them that the people at the U.N. were willing to become involved with others.

From there we went to what had impressed them during the day. (It should be noted that there was a great deal of discussion all during the trip and on the bus trip coming back.) After

101

some routine discussion I asked them about the problem of strengthening the U.N. This created considerable comment back and forth on the possibility, the advisability, the necessity, and the methods involved. We did not resolve the issue.

Monday, May 30. Memorial Day; school holiday.

Wednesday, June 1. With only four class days remaining, I decided it must be concerned with St. John's Gospel. My original outline was as follows for these days:

Take purpose of Gospel—"that you may believe that Jesus is the Christ, the Son of God, and that believing you may have life in his name."
Analysis of "life in his name." Take ideas of life including life in community. Elements of community, e.g., initiation, strengthening, common goals, unity. Take ideas of new community, the new creation in John versus old community, Old Testament. Then to idea of Christ as life and light of the new community.

The actual first session went something like this: *in his name* meant "born through him," "patterned after him," "life because of him," "grace," "spiritual life," etc. I asked what is this life and the answers included grace, spiritual life, supernatural life, charity, love. One student arrived at the answer that I was looking for, and that was life with community. I asked what were the elements involved in this community. The answers were: common purpose, leader, rules, common background. From there I went to the outline of the gospel given in the Collegeville series by Fr. Raymond Brown showing how Christ was establishing a new community. From there to John 3 and "born again" or "born from above" with Nicodemus. I asked them what was involved in being a member of the Jewish community. They answered in terms of circumcision and the Law. Then the bell rang.

Thursday, June 2. I opened the class by going back to John 3 on being born again or from above. I asked what this meant. One answer was a whole new approach to life. Another said giving up sensual pleasures. When I asked if the latter was good, one student said you had more freedom when you were a pagan. Another said being born again was a long-term investment rewarded in heaven. The student who felt paganism was more free then interjected a comment about Dr. Billy Graham, whom he listens to at times. He felt that Graham was interesting. When questioned why, he finally arrived at the idea of Graham being more demanding, the idea of giving your life to Christ. Graham was different from people you usually hear; he's convinced. Yet the same student felt that you could "hack around" more as a pagan. I asked, then, what appeal St. Paul had for the pagans in the early Church who were free to "hack around" and who followed Christ. He (the student) then commented that what I hear from Billy Graham I hear from Christ, i.e., an ideal. Another student interrupted here to say that paganism deals with self (he is implying a certain type of paganism which we didn't specify), while the Christian's demand is to the other. One student said Dorothy Day is alive; we're half-hearted. Other reasons for being born from above or again were given in terms

103

of heaven or reward. Many did not accept this. Another student said that a pagan might see love in another human being, and then be attracted to Christ as a result.

From here I went to a question of whether there is anything in the Christian religion that appeals to man. The answer was that it was a way of life that is satisfying. (This answer came from one student who was very much concerned during the entire discussion.) The bell rang at this point.

Monday, June 6. The rector gave an afternoon holiday in honor of his twenty-fifth anniversary of ordination.

Tuesday, June 7. Class Mass. On June 6, a student of this class found out that his brother had been killed in Vietnam. The class Mass was offered for that intention; we used the vestments of the day since the student did not feel it necessary to have the Requiem. The students prepared the prayer of the faithful; they gathered more fully around the altar; the kiss of peace was expressed by a handshake given around the class.

Wednesday, June 8. This was the last class. I had announced at the Mass that there would be no final examination. This had been cleared with the chairman of the religion department, the prefect of studies, and the rector. Both Fr. Richardson and I felt that it was unnecessary in view of the approach we had followed. Also at the lunch period after Mass yesterday I asked the students to fill out a questionnaire on the course. Out of the 34 distributed, 24 were returned.

For the last class I continued the discussion from the previous week. One student, in particular, had asked that we continue. He raised the question of whether we can reject baptism or not. He felt if we rejected baptism, having a choice, we could have freedom without guilt. I asked him what freedom he wanted. It was freedom to "hack around." I asked him what that meant. Did he mean it in terms of sexual morality. He said a pagan is happier because he could have sexual freedom without feeling any qualms. This raised, in a very brief fashion, the question of whether the pagan had any rules or restrictions on the use of sex. The question was raised whether sex was a personal or social phenomenon. Somewhere, at this point, I interpolated the idea that Christ had come that we might have life and have it more abundantly. The student who had raised the whole problem came up with the question of Hugh Hefner of *Playboy* magazine who has indicated that it seems unusual that Congress, for example, should have the power to bind social or moral legislation. I countered with the question of pornography. I asked why some communities object to pornography if sex is left to the individual completely.

We worked around to a certain extent on this area. I introduced the idea of what Good News is, since we were heading to the end of the period. One student said it was that the kingdom of God is here. The person Christ came down to give us eternal life. I mentioned the idea of union in John 6. This brought up the idea that the individual has to work to make this life come alive. The last note in my book says we have the freedom to love. (A student came to see me later in the day to continue the discussion on the meaning of the Christian life.)

105

Conclusion. The questionnaire below seems to indicate that the students who responded reacted well. What of the 10 who did not? How objective were the ones who did? Over-all view was that they learned and shared experiences. The experiences together were extremely valuable to them. The use of contemporary topics seemed to have been meaningful. In terms of content there seems to have been, from my point of view, enough.

My own reaction was one of guarded enthusiasm for the class. I enjoyed working with them and found it demanded a great amount of time in preparation and follow-up with these notes. (These notes have been invaluable in following the students' thoughts and directions.) I see weaknesses in too much time in some areas and not enough in others. I see the necessity for motivating the students to read more on their own, but I would not want to introduce graded assignments or examinations. The next class coming up will read *Christians Around the Altar*[1] over the summer. That should help in the background for liturgy. The students need more background in scripture. The lesson for me is to teach without the book, using materials for resource, but making the lesson come from them in connection with the general theme of the year.

Next year I am to use Fr. Vincent Novak's volume 4, *Christian Witness.* Looking it over, I think I will use it at resource, but not as a regular text.

In a few days I hope to meet with Fr. Richardson to go over the year and evaluate it more critically.[2]

1. Community of St. Severin, Notre Dame, 1961.
2. The time for formal discussion never materialized. Both Fr. Richard-

EVALUATION OF RELIGION CLASS

I would appreciate your assistance in helping me evaluate, as objectively as possible, the course we have gone through together. It is not a question of hurting the feelings of the teacher, or falsely boosting his feelings. In catechetics, it is important that teachers know strengths and weaknesses in teaching, in approach, in materials.

You do not have to sign your name on this sheet.

A. The theme of the year was community. Was it worthwhile?

    1. Yes _____ 2. Partially _____
    3. No _____
    4. If answered partially or no, please give reasons. _____

    _____

    _____

    5. What other possible themes could we use for a fourth-year
       course? _____

    _____

B. We used three basic texts: The Gospel of St. John, *Pacem in Terris,* and the Constitution on the Liturgy.
    6. Would you repeat these (if we repeated the same theme)?
       Yes _____ No _____

son and I were caught up taking courses in summer school which began immediately after school closed. I shared this journal with him and several other teachers, but a full exploration of difficulties did not come about, unfortunately.

In the fall, when we began planning for the new semester, we did adopt volume 4 of Fr. Novak's series, completing the cycle for the four year high school program here.

7. Which one or ones would you drop? _____

_____

_____

8. Why? _____

_____

C. We utilized two films, a speaker, and several trips, plus the class Mass.

9. What was your general reaction to the films? _____

_____

10. Specifically *The Neighbors?* _____

_____

11. *The Nightwatch?* _____

_____

12. What other films might you suggest? Why? _____

_____

_____

13. I know your reaction to Sr. Thomas Marie. Do you think we should consider repeating her, if we follow the same theme? Yes _____ No _____

14. Do you have any suggestions for other speakers? Please give names or fields from which speakers could be drawn.

_____

_____

15. What is your general reaction to speakers? _____

_____

16. We took two major trips, plus several small group excursions. What is your general reaction?

_____

_____

17. Regarding St. Ann's, what were the values you learned to appreciate? _____

_____

_____

18. What suggestions would you make for this type of trip?

_____

_____

19. Regarding the United Nations, what were the values you learned to appreciate? _____

_____

_____

20. Any suggestions for other field trips or areas you would want to explore (if you are thinking of a different theme for a year, please give theme and the suggested field trips)?

_____

_____

_____

21. The class Mass. Its values. _____

_____

22. Any suggestions about the class Mass. _____

_____

_____

D. Tone of the class. In this I am trying to evaluate the basic approach in a senior religion class. Your answers can be extremely valuable in my own evaluation of how I should be heading.

23. Answer one. Was the over-all pattern

more intellectual than devotional _____

more devotional than intellectual _____

relatively balanced intellectually and devotionally _____

109

24. Answer one:
    more information than formation _____
    more formation than information _____
    relatively balanced between information and formation _____
25. Answer one:
    more religious than secular _____
    more secular than religious _____
    relatively balanced between secular and religious _____
26. Did it come off as a religion class? Please explain your answer.

    _____
    _____
    _____

E. There were three major areas of material to be covered in the theme of community. They were unequal in treatment and time.
27. Liturgy: general reaction. _____

    _____

28. Suggestions. _____

    _____

29. *Pacem in Terris:* general reaction. _____

    _____
    _____

30. Suggestions. _____

    _____
    _____

31. St. John's Gospel: general reaction. _____

    _____
    _____

32. Suggestions. _____

    _____
    _____

F. Examinations and papers. We have kept written work and examinations to a minimum.
   33. Any advantages? _____
   34. Any disadvantages? _____
   35. Do you think you worked more or less because of less written work and assignments? Explain.

   _____
   _____
   _____

   36. Do you feel it would have been more profitable if you had been assigned more work?

   _____

G. What more do you think should have been done in this course?

   _____
   _____
   _____

H. How would you like more involvement of other teachers in classroom discussion? Explain.

   _____
   _____
   _____

I. Teacher's technique.
   37. Was there too much lecture? Yes _____
       No _____
   38. Was there sufficient freedom for thought and expression?
       Yes _____ No _____
   39. What would you suggest to the teacher in terms of classroom technique? _____

   _____
   _____

111

J. What would you want included in a fourth-year course?

40. _____

_____

_____

41. Third-year course? _____

_____

_____

42. Second-year course? _____

_____

_____

43. First-year course? _____

_____

_____

44. Any additional comments, please include below.

Thanks.

THE MEANING AND DIFFICULTIES OF
THE CATECHETICAL EXPERIENCE:
A REFLECTION

Since I have kept a journal of my religion class, I have become more and more conscious of the tensions and difficulties facing me as a religion teacher today. The relatively objective account from class to class has forced me to look at myself, my reactions, and to discover from and with others what is happening in my own and other teachers' classrooms.

I am not as assured of simple solutions as I might have been earlier in my years as a teacher. This is good if it challenges me, rather than discourages me. It can be healthy if it forces me to reflection rather than resignation. It is productive when it provides new insights rather than somewhat outmoded and lifeless formulas.

The basic tensions have partially and still come for me and other teachers from the fear of the unknown. Up to a few years ago, we knew what we had when students answered questions and completed graded examinations. We knew we had completed our work when we covered the material in the textbooks. In Confraternity of Christian Doctrine work, we often complained that we did not have time to cover the material, or that the material was inadequate; but the goal was the same—finish the text.

All this presumed that faith was fed and nourished, somewhat automatically, like a balanced diet which worked whether or not the person liked the food. The assimilation of material was sufficient to carry on the process of growth. Other factors may have entered into the process, but they were somewhat beyond the pale of the teacher: the family, background, the neighborhood, the social climate, the parish. Yet the role of the teacher was fairly clear, cover the material, and that eased the mind and heart of the teacher. The faith was so great that anyone would automatically accept it if he heard about it.

Now we are not as certain that the faith-by-feeding method is the answer. Even more, we are not as certain as to where we are heading and this uncertainty troubles us. We do not always want to take the risk of leaving our security; we do not always want to depart from the conventional way. This is due partially to wisdom in holding on to what is rich and valid; partially it is timidity or stagnation because we do not see that some of what we have been holding onto may be lifeless.

These are not absolutes or universals. Much has been done in the way of new growth in catechetics, but still there is uncertainty and tension. For many teachers these tensions are unsettling because there seems to be a chasm between ourselves and our students at times. It seems to be more than a generational gap, wherein time and experience would give the students the wisdom we have; but a new searching, a questioning (seeming like defiance) which has students asking us not what to believe, but why to believe, or why do we believe.

This can bring havoc to a teacher accustomed to discussion, perhaps even dialogue, on points in question, but who presumed that everyone agreed on the basic points. A religion teacher usually presumes belief, fairly solid but undeveloped. All that need be done is to develop that faith, that solid rock underlying everyone's question.

We generally presupposed that the gift of faith at baptism was never lost, but was always nourished and developed by each new contact with a priest, sister, brother, layman teaching CCD. It was increased with each reception of the sacraments, given support through the parish or school activities.

It was a comforting thought; it was a comfortable world. Yet somewhere the pattern has changed and we are looking anew (and occasionally with terror) at the new patterns emerging.

It is not a question as to whether faith is given at baptism. We are discovering in a way new to our times (although always implicit before) that faith is a human response, or better a *personal* response. This has raised questions now of personal development, maturity, freedom; it has challenged the automatic absorption, the unquestioning or unquestionable values; it has introduced the freedom to take a risk, the search for meaning, the restructuring of institutions to meet the person, the search for identity.

All this has affected those of us who teach, those who observe, those who are taught. We are and are not in a new faith. We have the same creed, the same Christ, the same Church. Yet we have perhaps seen new insights or new approaches to this same creed, Christ, and Church. We are in growth and yet growth can be painful to some of us because we were not told to expect it, because it involves moving from the secure land where faith and security are still meaningful for us, to the land of the younger generation still looking for meaning.

We are partially in a time when the young do not want to live in our land where we are at home, but want to go to a new land that seems more fertile and productive. The problem is that they may be right, that our land is becoming sterile and that we are being led on a new exodus.

The Second Vatican Council called us a pilgrim Church, but pilgrimages demand a willingness to go forward and to search long and strange paths. It demands faith, but there are two kinds of faith involved here: the faith of the young which believes in the unknown, the possible; the faith of the older ones which still perhaps longs for the unknown and the possible, but which is tempered by age and experience, which seeks security rather than escape, which feels it has arrived at a view of the pilgrim's goal and can rest.

These two faiths are meeting more and more in conflict. Yet it is a conflict of confusion, of anxiety, of tears. One group reaches out to the other and says come and share the richness of the Lord who has given us life. Follow our way of acceptance and docility (with some guarded questioning and challenge) and you will be blessed. The other group says we will come willingly when we are ready, when we have tasted and experimented, when we have seen and tasted for ourselves.

There is not necessarily an answer to this impasse. Our times seem to be one of major upheaval. What are needed, perhaps, are not answers, but reflections, questions, and observations. The easiest way out would be to presume that the tension today is one that will pass. The most dangerous path would be to accept this widescale upheaval as a passing phenomenon and ignore the times. Signs of life, questions which should be heard, acceptance of the times we live in, all require an open hearing. We learn because we hear. Perhaps we have much to hear today. Perhaps we are being called to a new land. We would be remiss if we did not remain open to the call.

A teacher of religion today is in a privileged situation. If he is open to himself and to his students (without necessarily losing his own identity in them), he gains a view of a world that, while still limited, seeks anew for meaning, mission, identity. Yet, for some of us in our twenties, thirties, and forties, this new world is a world not circumscribed by an established structure, a known way of life, a definite pattern of existence bounded by traditional society. It is, in its own way, a "brave new world." It is a world we had hoped for when we were younger, but one whose full dimensions we never realized. It is a world where man wants to be personally free, demanding new structures in order that the person may be free.

As teachers, we traditionally represent the established patterns and our role has usually been that of transmitter of the known norms in a fashion that would permit our students to enter into a known social or religious structure. Now this role seems to be disappearing and we are called to be pilgrims with our students rather than pilgrim directors watching from afar.

Pope John XXIII understood man's problem when he said of

the Church that "she must ever look to the present, to the new conditions and new forms of life introduced into the modern world, which have opened new avenues to the Catholic apostolate." Equally important is the idea that the Church is still "journeying in a foreign land away from her Lord, and regards herself to be in exile." This image of the Church offers a view of ourselves that challenges security, that places us again in the search for our place in the contemporary world. It is a call to look at where we are and where we are going rather than to look only at where we have been and where we should rest.

What all this requires of a teacher is a new look at aims and structures, methods and techniques. Basically, it calls for a reorientation of the meaning of faith for ourselves and our students, a restudy of what it means to be or to become a believer. This can be disturbing, but it can be rewarding. An immigrant group remains in the ghetto for strength and support, for protection and warmth, for its own vision of the world. It needs its structures in order that the life within can be nourished and prepared for the world around it. But it eventually must go forth and meet the world around it since it cannot, over the long run, avoid the outside world without impoverishing itself. Also it eventually learns and grows from its limited contacts with that outside world. The ghetto is the womb which gives life, but which also creates dependence and a false sense of security.

Within our own community today, we must also be willing to break forth and, as it were, give up the security and protection of our walls and that for two reasons: we are called to go forth by our very nature; and our younger generation is ready and willing and eager to meet that new world. We cannot keep them within the womb, for they were made for life itself.

There are, of course, dangers in leaving the established community and its norms. Yet man in finding his identity does not have to lose his roots; his identity should include them. The danger is in not having man find his own identity and substituting the community for his identity. When and if pushed to the test, a man who has not found his own identity in himself, through the help of the community, may find it without the community he was raised in.

The risk for teachers today is in allowing our students to find their own identities, not through the community's structure, but through the community's help. Our students are the generation that is ready to leave the womb of the structure; in fact, the womb is ready to give them life. Occasionally, we are like a fearful midwife, afraid that the labor pains are too early and unwilling to assist at the birth.

For our generation, it is true, the pattern of new life was clearly defined in all areas. Our society defined its limits, its aims, its criteria of success or failure. Our schools and curriculum changed slowly, as is common in institutions. But outside the institutional walls, developments pushed ahead. Many in the community of the Church were aware; but security was more acceptable and meaningful than "awareness" which could challenge and upset the community.

The new birth that is occurring is not as awesome as it may first appear. Community structures are necessary if man is to survive; yet it is also possible that they can be fossilized, can be inert, can be lifeless rather than life-giving and sustaining. Community structure can demand that the individual give up his self-consciousness because the community has lost its own self-consciousness. It can demand that the individual no longer be a person because the community has ceased to be a community of persons. When that has happened, new birth may be needed if life is to go on.

We have always been the people of God; yet the history of this people has always been one of renewal, or re-identification. It has always been incarnational, finding itself within a cultural pattern that opened up new forms for God to be present to man. We are still that people of God, but perhaps we have not realized the need for renewal that has come upon us. Man tends to look back upon Egypt as a comforting place when he is in Sinai. Now we are looking back, not necessarily to Egypt, but to the last place of peace and quiet we have just left on our journey in exile.

Birth requires a new view of the world outside the womb. Our students are doing that today. They are discovering that the world outside the Christian community can be good; that the ghetto rules are not necessarily the only ones; that their parents in the faith are, at times, clinging to the community structures they needed and which they want to impose on them.

This is the area of tension. We parents in the faith realize the dangers for the young and in our wisdom want to help them mature; the young, being young, do not necessarily want to identify with our generation. What is lacking today is the insight needed by the older group in order to understand the view of the young, to be willing to let them go forth, not unaided and alone, but together with us into the new world where we are all called to live. For ourselves, the older group, it may be a strange land with new signs and languages, but we bring to it the richness of our background. For the young, it is a world in which they will need the richness of the older generation for true support, for the necessary essentials needed to search out a strange land.

What a person believes in is frequently conditioned by what his society is and what he knows. For people of fairly highly structured lives, belief can be fairly easy to establish. For a person in transit, belief becomes more and more personal and de-institutionalized since it is not supported by the society he is in. One of the areas that disturbs teachers today is the question of belief on the part of students. It is no longer the unquestioning acceptance, but more the challenge, the personal search. Perhaps it is because they are looking at a new world and their eyes see things we do not see. Perhaps it is because we have stopped looking as closely at the world around us, preferring our own view. (It is interesting to note that some liberals of the thirties, forties, and early fifties have become fairly conservative in their thinking.)

Yet what has happened in all this is a rethinking of how a man views the world, how he makes an act of faith, how man grows in relation to himself and the world around him and God. From our understanding now of our role as pilgrims, we see that faith is not static but dynamic, that it is involved in personal growth, that it is not as definite as some of our cultural norms were, that "it is not something we have, but something that we win everyday."

Perhaps some teachers will be more at ease if we realize that the act of faith, which some students seem to challenge by their questions and attitudes, is not a static act. What does it mean to be Christian? Is it a state, a *fait accompli,* or is it to become, to go continually in the direction of Christ? It is a searching, a continual meeting of the person to the person of Christ with all the difficulties inherent in the personal meeting, with the uncertainty of personal encounter. It is not that personal meeting with Christ is erratic, but that it involves the difficulties inherent in the meeting of person to person.

Leslie Dewart, in *The Future of Belief,* comments on the meaning of faith and of questioning and difficulty in a Christian when he writes:

. . . [regarding] the meaning of unfaithfulness to the Christian faith —I mean, the unfaithfulness that every Christian's true faith *must* suffer. I have in mind the constant, never ending active effort which faith requires under pain of decline, that is, the need for perpetual renewal and growth which corresponds to the faith's always falling short of itself. For belief does not take place in an "act"—even if some moments of one's religious life are more vital than others. For faith is always coming-into-being, it is never quite fully faithful, it is always on the way, hence never perfect and achieved.[1]

Of course, the objections may be raised that this should not be the situation for our students, that they should accept before they reject, that they must be formed so that they can have

1. New York, 1966, p. 64.

standards by which to judge. Also there is the question of whether every man is capable of this type of conscious activity.

Yet underlying these criticisms is the basic question of faith as a dynamic act which, perhaps, is not simply formed but, depending on time and circumstances for many, becomes a process of growth rather than a state of being. In our own age, as the cultural patterns supporting faith tend to lessen, faith may not be the culturally static support, but may require the sense of "unfaithfulness" in order to become. Perhaps a future age will be different; our age presents the challenge of "becoming."

The catechetical experience today, seen in the context of faith becoming, has its own difficulties. What in this new land is common and valid for the learned and the learning? Does the learning process become a sharing of insights, the one from the past, the other of the present and the future? Who will lead?

In this view, the roles of the teacher and student take on new relationships, and they are not necessarily easy ones to define. Father Pierre Babin in his books *Options* and *Methods* treats the role of the teacher in terms of a fraternal relationship, less authoritarian, and more guiding. Implied in this approach is a willingness on the part of the teacher to be part of the search in the new land with his students, providing them with the resources he has from age and background; yet, at the same time, he must be willing to learn from new experiences.

For many, both teachers and students, this new role will be disconcerting. Certitude is a highly praised and valued need, yet we are required to take uncertain steps, because we see something dimly ahead which beckons us. As adults, and even as students, we do not always want to leave the certainty we have unless there is a vision that calls us forth.

This is where the elements of vision and faith meet. We must realize that we are called forth, that certitude is perhaps an eschatological factor, something to come, that our call to abundance of life means growth, movement, even uncertainty, that, as Dewart has said, "we cannot believe in God once-for-all any more than we can exist once-for-all" (page 65).

Does this rule out certainty, authority, stability? Yes, in the sense that the pilgrim has no clear view of his goal, but it implies more: "The 'certitude' of faith is of the sort that allows, rather *requires* uncertainty. This does not mean, on the other hand, that faith can be described as a sort of doubt. It means that the Christian faith excludes *belief* in the truth of belief. This is why faith seeks to surpass itself precisely as faith. That is, it seeks what it has not, and insofar as it seeks truth it speculates. In any event, the point is that the Christian is not permitted to have faith: he may have faith only in God" (Dewart, page 70).

Yet in all this we must return to the student, the one who is learning in some way, if even by question; who is discovering in his challenges; who even grows perceptive through his doubts. Goldbrunner says that the true growth of a faith received through others "is limited to the period of man's growth from infancy to maturity, in which period the possibilities of incarnation of faith and of pastoral care stand or fall, even though there are no limits to the exceptional effects of grace."[1] The same idea was

1. J. Goldbrunner, *Realization: The Anthropology of Pastoral Care,* Notre Dame, 1966, p. 61.

expressed by Eusebius of Caesarea when he said, "What we learn as a youth grows with our soul and is part of us."

The process of discipline needed in growth, of the role of habit in religious formation, cannot be ignored (cf. Goldbrunner, *Realization,* especially Chapter VII), and if it is ignored, that is done so at the expense of the right of the student to be developed. What we must be aware of is the right of the student also to be accepted as he is today and then to be prepared to work with him.

It can be frightening to a teacher to have his own beliefs and assumptions challenged. Part of our difficulty today may lie in our unwillingness to rethink vocabulary, concepts, our own traditions; to be unwilling to take the risk of Pope John XXIII when he asked us to look to the new life around us. Man tends to look to his homeland with longing and also nostalgia, even if the reality was not all he actually desired or had. But at least he knew what it was. In religious education today we are not asked to give up or give in. We are asked to look about and discover what is meaningful and valid in the contemporary world.

Can this be done and still inculcate in our students the knowledge and habits needed in their time of growth? Yes, but perhaps in different structures, structures of honest and frank exchange, even of refusal at times. Discovery involves study and the habit of intellectual discipline, and it will take time for more recognizable structures to evolve where we will feel more comfortable.

Yet we must not strive simply towards a sense of security, for we belong to a pilgrim Church and are always on our way *towards.* We move constantly deeper into new terrain, and must always seek to discern new signs of direction. With each new step we must stop and discover where we are, but we cannot rest or settle down for long. Our greatest security, our assurance that we will reach our goal, lies in our faltering but never-ceasing forward steps.